organisms, behaviour and health

key stage three

teaching the *right* science at the *right* time

author Jo Locke

editor Roger Ellis

series editor Ken Gadd

science

Design and publisher

4science
6 The Courtyard, Dean's Farm
Stratford sub Castle
Salisbury, Wiltshire
SP1 3YP

www.4science.org.uk

Images

www.photos.com (Jupiter Images)

(unless otherwise stated)

Printed in Great Britain

JMD Print Management
3 Miles's Buildings, George Street, Bath BA1 2QS
www.jmd-print.co.uk

About the books

This series of books has been written for all science teachers. No matter what scheme of work you are using, whether you are teaching by science topic or cross-curriculum theme, the books in this series will provide you with invaluable support. We hope that, over time, your books will become well thumbed, dog-eared and annotated; in other words, well used.

The series is based on a simple philosophy – the need to teach the *right science* at the *right time*.

Scientific ideas and concepts are introduced, developed and expanded over an educational journey that spans at least eleven years of a young person's life. Many go beyond this time frame. Often, concepts are revisited, reviewed and taken forward. Models of matter and change, for example, become more sophisticated. This does not mean that earlier models were 'wrong'. A model is as good as its predictive power. If something unexpected crops up which the model is unable to explain, we revisit and refine it. On occasions we start again with a new model.

So, this book's first message to teachers is: show Key Stage 3 pupils how scientific ideas, concepts and models emerge, how they are tested experimentally and how they are refined or adjusted if necessary. Pupils should not think simpler models are 'wrong'. We need to develop the complexity in parallel with a pupil's intellectual development.

Along the way, pupils may bring with them alternative conceptions of why the world we live in is the way it is. This does not mean they are wrong, rather that their experiences may render new ideas counter-intuitive. Often, we label these as misconceptions – and we need to help pupils over these barriers as quickly as possible. Failure to do so may present an obstacle to learning that takes far more time than it should to break down.

The second message is: confront misconceptions as early as possible. The book identifies commonly held misconceptions and offers suggestions for how they might be overcome. This cannot be comprehensive or exhaustive, but we hope it is useful and, indeed, helps trigger other ideas.

A further barrier to learning can be the language and terminology we use in science, especially where the meaning of a term used in everyday life is rather different to its meaning when used in a scientific situation. A political situation may be volatile, but that doesn't mean it has a low boiling point (though you can see the relationship).

The third message Is: use the language and terminology of science correctly and precisely.

It is debatable whether there is such a thing as a 'scientific method'. Rarely is scientific discovery a linear process. There is much back tracking, rethinking and retesting. Nonetheless, rigorous scientific approaches to tackling problems characterise good science. It is the essence of good experimental design and data interpretation.

The fourth message is: ensure pupils understand how science works. Pupils should question, challenge and not take everything at face value (do anti-wrinkle creams really work?).

There are other messages that will emerge as you use the book. They will all help you to teach the right science at the right time.

Ken Gadd
Series Editor

contents

other titles in this series

- chemical and material behaviour
- earth, environment and the universe
- energy, electricity and forces
- interpreting how science works

using this book

The book covers the range and content of *organisms, behavious and health* in the Science Programme of Study for Key Stage 3.

Topics are arranged in chapters, with the relevant science given on the first double page of each.

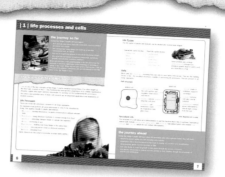

the journey so far

Every chapter begins with information about what pupils are likely to have learnt before coming to secondary school, or previously in Key Stage 3.

The primary curriculum is not highly prescriptive; pupils will arrive at secondary school having been taught science of varying degrees of complexity and depth. You will find here a summary of the prior knowledge, skills and understanding that you can reasonably expect pupils to have.

the science at key stage 3

The appropriate science for the topic at Key Stage 3 is encapsulated in the main content of this double page. Some terms are highlighted. Pupils should have a good understanding of these, to have a full grasp of the science being taught and to be able to progress.

Science teachers, whatever their discipline, have considerable knowledge and understanding; this section pinpoints what is necessary for 11-14 year olds. The terminology, approach, and explanations of facts and concepts are aimed at fostering clarity in your understanding and support for your teaching. The phraseology may not always be suitable for use with pupils; it does not provide a 'script' for lessons. You will also have to consider how much of the topic is suitable for the year group and ability range of the class. Your own words, style and lesson plan are still needed.

Presented here is the underpinning to that sound level of science which, building on learning at Key Stage 2, will meet the requirements of Key Stage 3 and prepare pupils for the journey ahead.

the journey ahead

This section indicates the related science that pupils will encounter as they progress to Key Stage 4 science (or allied subjects) and beyond.

It makes the continuum explicit; the science taught at this stage should provide the correct framework for the next stage of learning.

After the opening double page, each chapter deals with the principal concerns when teaching the topic:

- teaching issues
- applications and implications

... as well as one or more of:

- history and culture
- hot topics
- facts and figures.

teaching issues

This main section has further coverage of the science content at a level that extends beyond what pupils need to know. It provides a knowledge base from which you should be able to teach comfortably.

It varies from chapter to chapter but, generally, there are suggestions about when best to teach the topic, common problems and difficulties when teaching the topic, and suggestions for practical activities and demonstrations.

How science works permeates this and other sections. However, there are some basic tools that pupils use that are not covered in depth in this book, for example, units, symbols and graph drawing. These are covered in the companion volume *interpreting how science works*, together with explanations of the other key processes and concepts, and their application within Key Stage 3.

Sub-sections include:

Vocabulary and language

Pupils encounter a mass of new and bewildering terminology while learning science. Much of it is new. Pupils will also have encountered slang and inappropriate words. Such terminology is highlighted and ways of dealing with it are suggested.

Misconceptions

Many pupils pick up misconceptions which they can carry throughout their education, unless put straight. Attention is drawn to common misconceptions and useful ideas for quashing them are provided.

Questions

Pupils like to ask questions and are encouraged to do so. Sometimes they are questions to which you may not readily know the answers, particularly if you are not teaching your specialist subject. Some of those questions – and their answers – are here.

> *Suggested activities*
>
> *Throughout the book, there are possible pupil activities – such as practical work, literacy tasks, debates, presentations, etc. – which can aid your teaching. They are not step by step instructions but, rather, suggestions. These sorts of activities can easily be seen as you flick through the book; they are written in orange boxes with an orange border, like this one.*

applications and implications

This is a discussion about applications and implications of the science – be it science in the home or science in the workplace. The ethics of scientific and technological discovery and methods are touched on, where this is an issue.

history and culture

As the heading suggests, this section contains some notes on historical or cultural aspects of the topic.

Such data can form the basis of activities that illustrate how science works, as well as providing interesting insights.

hot topics

Science is not, of course, all about what has already happened. Its very nature is one of discovery. Some of the cutting edge science – the sorts of things that make the newspapers – is here. However, unlike the newspapers, the aim is not to sensationalise but to demystify.

facts and figures

Useful (or, at least, very interesting) facts and figures give additional colour and inform pupils and colleagues alike. They can also be difficult to find, unless gathered neatly in one place, as here, in this section.

| 1 | life processes and cells

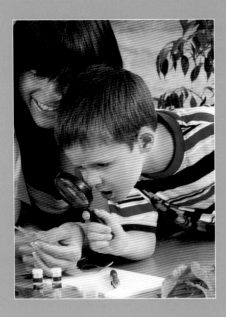

the journey so far

During Key Stage 2, pupils should have learnt:

*   that animals and plants have life cycles with common distinct processes and stages
*   the concept that living things are made up of smaller components such as organs
*   the use of magnifying glasses to see small structures clearly
*   the seven life processes (movement, respiration, sensitivity, growth, reproduction, excretion, nutrition).

Many will not have a full understanding of the life processes: for example, a common explanation of the meaning of excretion is 'going to the toilet'. Many will not have used a microscope. Cells are not part of the primary curriculum and are introduced for the first time in this Key Stage 3 topic.

the science at key stage 3

Cells is one of the key concepts at Key Stage 3 and is revisited several times. It is often taught as the first topic covered in Year 7. This fundamental concept then progresses on to cellular organisation (tissues, organs and organ systems responsible for carrying out the fundamental life processes).

The ethics and potential uses of stem cell research are important applications and implications of modern science.

Life Processes

There are seven life processes common to all living organisms.

An organism must perform all seven processes in order to be classified as living. This applies equally to plants and animals.

*   Movement – moving themselves (or parts of themselves) without external help
*   Respiration – using chemical reactions to release energy from food
*   Sensitivity – detecting changes inside or outside the organism
*   Growth – increasing in size
*   Reproduction – making new living things of the same kind
*   Excretion – removing waste made in chemical reactions
*   Nutrition – obtaining food

(Note: these form the easy-to-remember acronym **MRS GREN**.)

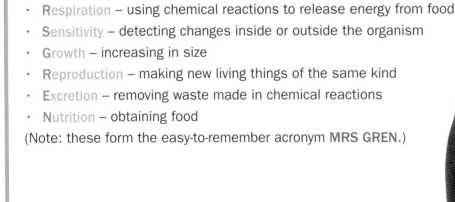

Life Cycles

The life cycles of plants and animals can be divided into several main stages.

Animal life cycles involve:
- fertilisation
- birth
- growth
- adolescence
- reproduction

Plant life cycles involve:
- fertilisation
- seed dispersal
- germination
- growth
- pollination

Some animals also undergo metamorphosis (change from immature growth stage to adult), such as a butterfly or a frog.

Cells

Most cells are microscopic, meaning they can only be seen with a microscope. They are the building blocks of life – the smallest structures capable of performing life processes. They are present in all living organisms.

Cell structure

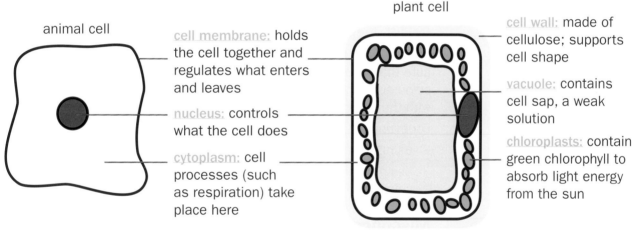

plant cell

animal cell

cell membrane: holds the cell together and regulates what enters and leaves

nucleus: controls what the cell does

cytoplasm: cell processes (such as respiration) take place here

cell wall: made of cellulose; supports cell shape

vacuole: contains cell sap, a weak solution

chloroplasts: contain green chlorophyll to absorb light energy from the sun

note: diagrams not to scale

Specialised cells

The structure of a cell alters as it differentiates to suit the function that it has to perform.
Specialised animal cells include: nerve, ovum (egg), sperm and red blood.
Specialised plant cells include: leaf palisade and root hair (which do not contain chloroplasts).

the journey ahead

During Key Stage 4, pupils will learn about life processes and cells in greater detail. They will study:
- structures present within the cell, including mitochondria
- inheritance (this is first introduced in this book in *chapter 11: variation and classification*)
- chromosomes, genes and the structure of DNA
- how cells divide, in order for growth to take place through the process of mitosis
- how genetic information is passed on from parents to their children, through the processes of meiosis and fertilisation.

teaching issues

Literacy task

Wordsearches, word-builder and crossword games are fun ways to practise and learn cell terminology.

Teaching sequence

A logical beginning is to build on learning at Key Stage 2 by looking at life processes and life cycles, as these are concepts with which pupils are familiar.

Vocabulary and use of language

Many pupils find cellular terminology hard to remember and the terms difficult to distinguish.

Often pupils use incorrect combinations of terms (for example, chloroplasm).

Pupils need to practise this vocabulary as frequently as possible, and should be provided with many opportunities to label structures and functions in a variety of cells.

Acronyms and mnemonics, like MRS GREN or MRS NERG for life processes, can be valuable memory aids.

Colour coding

Use a colour coding system to help pupils identify structures. Make sure that, in every diagram of a cell, the main structures are always coloured in the same colour. This constant repetition will aid pupils with their learning.

For example:

· using blue for vacuoles reinforces that they contain water
· using green for chloroplasts illustrates that they contain chlorophyll

Create your own ...

Make cell models to quash misconceptions. Use a variety of materials, such as modelling clay and egg boxes. Cardboard boxes can form rigid cell walls, and plastic food bags can form cell membranes. Fill the plastic bags with wallpaper paste to look and behave like cytoplasm.

Misconceptions

Misconception: Cells are flat 2D objects. Pupils find it very hard to visualize the three-dimensional structure of a cell as they are normally only shown as pictures, diagrams, through a microscope and so on, as a flat image.

Misconception: Structures within a cell don't move. It should be stressed that cells are dynamic – structures within the cell move around and are not static. So, even organisms like bacteria, that do not appear to move, show independent internal movements.

Misconception: All plant cells contain chloroplasts. Remind pupils that they can only work if light can reach them – so roots are not green.

Misconception: Every cell has a wall. Cell membranes are often confused with cell walls. Plant cells have cell walls, but animal cells do not. Emphasise the relatively fixed shape of plant cells and the flexible shape of animal cells.

Is a car a living thing?

Challenge pupils to explain why a car is not a living thing, using MRS GREN as their guide.

Questions to develop understanding

If making cell models, ask,

'How do the models differ from real cells?'

Using a microscope

Pupils often lack confidence and use microscopes ineffectively. Many pupils will have never had the opportunity to use a microscope. Some pupils find it difficult to see an image clearly through the eyepiece and many find it hard to focus microscopes. Pupils often have difficulty in recognising individual cells.

Good microscope skills

To aid pupils ...

- demonstrate correct use and provide clear instructions
- initially, use prepared slides with well defined specimens that are easy to focus on, to obtain a clear image (for example, well stained sections of sunflower stems)
- set up pre-focused microscopes or use bioviewers alongside their microscopes
- project and explain images of what to look for (using photomicrographs or a video microscope)
- emphasise the need not only to focus sharply, but also to illuminate well
- look down pupil microscopes to check they can see what is necessary
- maintain interest, build confidence and develop skills by allowing pupils to prepare their own simple specimens on slides for observation and to produce accurate drawings of their observations.

Increasing understanding

Pupils should study both plant and animal material to gain an understanding of the main differences and similarities of plant and animal cells.

To enthuse pupils and consolidate the understanding that they are made of cells, allow them to observe their own skin or cheek cells. At this stage, they need only recognise and explain simply the function of the nucleus, cell membrane, cytoplasm, cell wall, chloroplast and vacuole.

(Other structures will be introduced in Key Stage 4.)

Activity

Making measurements of cells can help pupils to develop an understanding of very small numbers. To do this pupils could use eyepiece graticules and stage micrometers.

Cell sizes

Pupils find it extremely difficult to understand the concept of how large a cell is. Time should be spent allowing pupils to observe known structures visible to the eye under the microscope – such as text on a page, grains of rice or human hair – to allow them to appreciate how small a cell actually is.

If graticules do not match the magnifying factor of a microscope eyepiece, stage micrometers can be used to graduate them. At lower magnification, a plastic ruler placed on the microscope stage can be used to measure the width of the field of view, and then cells can be compared with this. Ask pupils to decide how many cells are needed to fit across the width.

facts and figures

Cell size is a question regularly raised by pupils. It is a difficult question to answer as cells vary greatly in size.

Most cells, both animal and plant, range in size between 10 and 100 µm (10^{-5} to 10^{-4} m) and are thus visible only with the aid of a microscope.

By contrast, the nerve cells that run down a giraffe's neck can exceed three metres in length!

Human cells also display variety of size: small red blood cells measure 8 µm, whereas liver cells may be 10 times larger.

At both Key Stage 3 and Key Stage 4, a rough approximation to the size of a cell is enough. Therefore:

· a generic human cell is approximately 10 µm in diameter

· a generic plant cell is approximately 100 µm in diameter.

Pupils should not be expected to use micrometre at this stage, though this could be used to challenge and extend.

A simpler approach is to explain that about 100 typical human cells or 10 typical plant cells would line up on a 1 mm line.

About 10 000 average-sized human cells can fit on the head of a pin.

The existence of cells has been known about since the early seventeenth century when the microscope was developed.

Robert Hooke

In 1665, Robert Hooke, an English scientist, published his book *Micrographia*. It was full of carefully drawn pictures and descriptions of objects that cannot be seen clearly with the eye. In this book, Hooke described cork as being made up of 'a great many little boxes', which he called 'pores or cells', as it reminded him of the rooms that monks live in (taken from the Latin cellulae, meaning small rooms). From his examination of dead cork cells, Hooke was able to observe that thick walls surrounded each cell.

Schleiden, Schwann and Virchow

It was not until the nineteenth century when lenses were refined, making the microscope a more useful tool, that scientists fully realised that cells were the basis of life and therefore the building block of most living things.

In 1838, Matthias Schleiden, a German botanist, suggested that all plant tissues are made of cells. This was followed one year later by Theodore Schwann, a zoologist, who proposed that all animals are made up of cells.

In 1855, Rudolf Virchow developed his theory 'cellula e cellula' – that every cell stems from another cell. The accepted theory up until this time was the idea of the generation of cells by building them up from scratch.

The discoveries of these three scientists led to the development of modern cell theory; knowledge of cell structures and functions caused a fundamental shift in the way that biologists explained their findings.

A sketch of Hooke's microscope

Cell theory

Cell theory forms an intrinsic part of the study of cytology, histology, physiology and genetics.

The three main aspects of cell theory are:

1 All living things are composed of cells.
2 The chemical reactions that occur in an organism occur in cells.
3 All cells come from pre-existing cells.

At Key Stage 3, it is not necessary to consider such contradictions to cell theory as the syncytial structure (continuous cytoplasm with scattered nuclei) of skeletal muscle or placental epithelium. The ideas of cell theory seem obvious, but aspects of the details remain in dispute even today.

hot topics

Stem cells

Exciting advances in cell science are currently taking place in the field of stem cell research.

What are stem cells?

Stem cells are cells which have the ability to turn into other specialised types of cells. For example, a stem cell can turn (differentiate) into liver, skin or nerve cells. Stem cells originally divide in their undifferentiated state until they receive a signal which causes certain genes to be switched on, resulting in proteins being made. These proteins change the appearance and function of the cell into its new specialised state.

Types of stem cells

There are three main types of stem cell:

Embryonic stem cells

Found in the very early stages of a fertilised egg called a blastocyst. In a developing embryo, stem cells can differentiate into any kind of cell in the body. These are known as totipotent cells.

Adult stem cells

Found in tissues that have already developed and are therefore found in children as well as adults. They act as a repair system for the body, replenishing specialised cells, but also maintaining the normal turnover of regenerative tissues, such as blood, skin and intestinal epithelium. They are multipotent cells – they can produce only cells of a closely related family of cells. An example is bone marrow cells; these can produce a wide range of different blood cells.

Umbilical cord stem cells

Collected from the cells of the umbilical cord of a recently born baby. Some of these cells are slightly undeveloped and so can turn into other types of cells – they are multipotent.

Why are stem cells important?

Stem cells can be grown and transformed *in vitro* into specialised cells such as muscles or nerves through cell culture.

Stem cell therapy has the potential to change, dramatically, the treatment of many human diseases. The aim is to repair damaged tissues which do not heal naturally. Transplanted stem cells may be directed to grow new, healthy tissue. It may also be possible to stimulate stem cells already present in the body, to produce this new tissue.

A number of adult stem cell therapies exist now. The most well known is the use of bone marrow stem cells in a bone marrow transplant to treat leukaemia and other types of cancer and blood disorders. Medical researchers anticipate using stem cells to treat a wide variety of diseases including cancers, diabetes, brain diseases (such as Parkinson's disease), spinal cord injuries and muscle damage.

Much stem cell therapy relies on cells donated by another person. This carries an inherent risk of rejection by the recipient's immune system. Increasingly, it has become possible for a person to use a sample of their own stem cells to regenerate tissue, which considerably reduces the possibility of rejection occurring.

Research opportunity

Stem cell therapy is a key area of current scientific research. Pupils can look further into the use of stem cells in the treatment of leukaemia and Parkinson's disease.

applications and implications

Ethics

Advances in stem cell research and the activities of pressure groups constantly appear in the news. Ethical concerns may be raised by discussing topical issues. Present the arguments for and against a controversial issue such as stem cell research in an impartial manner. Some pupils may take extreme and opposing viewpoints – be aware of potential cultural and religious influences within your group.

Arguments for stem cell research

- Stem cells could potentially treat and cure many human diseases including Alzheimer's disease, diabetes, cancer, and strokes.
- An organ replacement is often difficult to obtain. Stem cell treatment could remove the reliance on donated organs, which require careful matching between donor and recipient.
- Stem cells may be taken from an embryo. Although the embryo has the potential to develop Into a baby, it may be argued that at this stage it is not a conscious organism, and therefore not yet human. Donated embryos (created for IVF treatment) which are not required for stem cells are otherwise destroyed. Use of these cells does not therefore destroy a potential life.

Arguments against stem cell research

- Many pro-life supporters believe that human life begins at the time of fertilisation between the ovum and the sperm. Thus, killing an embryo in order to extract its stem cells is a form of murder.
- Stem cell research could potentially lead to the formation of human clones.
- Unused embryos from UVF treatment are used for stem cell research – but this supply is not plentiful enough. Therefore, stem cell research would require the production of embryos to be killed solely for research.

Science club

Have pupils research stem cell issues and divide into 'for' and 'against' viewpoints. Problems facing modern scientific research can be highlighted as the debate progresses.

the journey so far

During Key Stage 2, pupils should have learnt to:

* name some organs present in plants (for example, leaf, flower, and root) and animals (for example, brain, heart and stomach)
* describe simply the functions of the main organs present in plants and animals
* locate the position of the main organs in plants and animals.

Some pupils may have an awareness that organs act together to perform a function, such as the stomach and intestines break down and absorb food. However, they will not be aware that organs can form systems like the digestive system.

Pupils will have been taught that there are two main categories of living things, plants and animals, but may not be familiar with the term organism.

the science at key stage 3

Some organisms, such as bacteria, are able to perform all life processes within a single cell. Multicellular organisms contain organ systems to perform their life processes. They have five layers of organisation of increasing complexity:

increasing complexity →

Organisms (for example, monkey)

Organ systems (for example, digestive system)

Organs (for example, small intestine)

Tissues (for example, intestine lining – epithelium)

Cells (for example, lining cell of intestine – an epithelial cell)

Cells are the building blocks – they appear as the bottom layer of organisation. Organisms are the most complex and hence form the final tier of the hierarchy.

Tissues

A tissue is a group of similar cells, working together to perform a particular function (job).

Examples of animal tissues include:

* muscle tissue – contracts to bring about movement
* nervous tissue – conducts electrical impulses
* lining of the intestine – absorbs nutrients

Examples of plant tissues include:

* phloem – carries sugars (sucrose)
* xylem – carries water and minerals from the soil

Organs

An organ is made up of a group of different tissues, working together to perform a specific function.

Animal organs and their functions include:

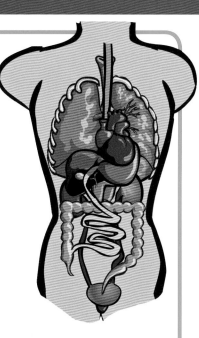

- heart – pumps blood around the body
- lungs – take in oxygen and remove carbon dioxide from the body
- liver – removes toxins from the blood; produces bile to aid digestion
- kidney – filters the blood; produces urine

Organs in a plant include:

- stem – holds the plant upright
- leaf – absorbs sunlight for making food (photosynthesis)
- root – anchors the plant and takes up water and minerals from the soil

Organ systems

An organ system is made up of a group of different organs, working together to perform a specific job. The human body has eight major organ systems:

- circulatory
- respiratory
- hormone
- movement (musculo-skeletal)
- digestive
- nervous
- reproductive
- excretory

They have specific functions, for example:

- circulatory – circulates blood, transporting materials to and from cells
- respiratory – takes in oxygen and removes carbon dioxide
- digestive – digests food and absorbs nutrients

Plant structure is much simpler and mainly organised at organ or tissue level. However, flowers form the reproductive system, and usually contain both male and female sex organs.

Organisms

Plants and animals are multicellular organisms made up of different organ systems working together. Other organisms, such as bacteria, can be single-celled.

the journey ahead

During Key Stage 4, pupils will learn about organs and organisms in greater detail. They will study:

- detailed functions of tissues, in particular the blood – including the different types of blood cells, and the specific roles they play in the immune system (this is first introduced in this book in *chapter 3: the circulatory system*)
- detailed functions of organs – for example how the kidney filters the blood, produces urine and the effect of anti-diuretic hormone (ADH) on this process.

teaching issues

Vocabulary and use of language

Key terms

There are five important terms in this topic – cells, tissues, organs, organ systems and organisms. Some pupils will find it difficult to remember the order of complexity.

Take opportunities to repeat words to help pupils to remember them.

Stress the hierarchy of the levels – each has something added to get a larger and larger structure. Ask questions such as:

'What is a tissue / organ / organ system / organism made out of?'

A diagram will help to reinforce this concept:

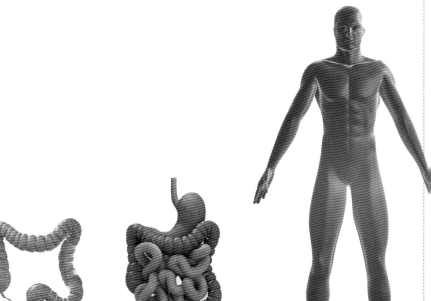

| cell level | tissue level | organ level | organ system level | organism level |

Card matching activity

Provide pupils with cards containing the names of some cells, tissues, organs, and organ systems. Have them sort the cards into the correct order – starting with a cell and ending with an organ system.

Muscle: tissue or organ?

The term muscle can be very confusing. Muscle tissue consists of cells that have the ability to shorten or contract. This causes movement of body parts.

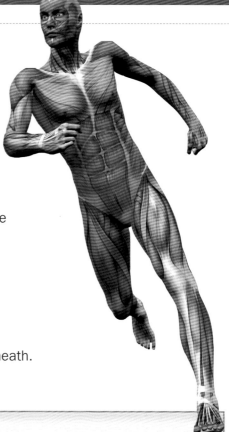

However, a whole skeletal muscle is considered an organ. Examples include the biceps and triceps muscles. As well as containing muscle tissue, the biceps contains connective tissue, nerve tissue and blood.

To aid pupil understanding, explain that the word 'muscle' is used in two different ways and discuss why a muscle (organ) needs more than just contracting cells to work. Ask, 'What does a muscle like your biceps need to work?' Use other questions to tease out the various functions of, and the need for, a range of tissues:

- oxygen and food to supply energy – blood vessels
- control of movement – nerves/nerve cells
- attachment to bones – tendons
- holding all the muscle tissues together – outer membrane or sheath.

Demonstration

Dissection is an excellent way to demonstrate that plants and animals are made of organs and organs are made of tissues. Use a chicken leg to show how muscle tissue is only part of a muscle organ.

Nerves and nerve cells

Nerves and nerve cells are also sometimes confused. Use this as another example of how organs are built up:

- a nerve cell (neurone) is used to send electrical signals
- nerve cells are bundled together to give nervous tissue
- more tissues are added (sheath of connective tissue and blood vessels) to form the nerve - an organ.

Functions

Results of (now defunct) SATs (Levels 5-9) showed that many pupils do not understand what function means. It is important that they learn its meaning as 'what something does' or its 'job'.

Help pupils gain familiarity with the term function by using it often. At first, explain its meaning by also using simpler language at the same time. For example:

'The function, or job, of the kidney is to filter blood and make urine.'

When pupils have become used to you using the word function with an explanation, test them by asking questions about the functions of tissues, organs or organ systems. For example:

'What is the function of your heart?'

Activity

*To familiarise pupils with the use of the term **function** and to help them associate structures and their functions, prepare a set of cards with named tissues, organs and systems. Make a second set of functions (for example, labelled 'Function: absorbs nutrients'). Use the cards to play 'snap' for a matching structure and function turned over together.*

Misconceptions

Misconception: Humans and animals are different. Some pupils at the start of Key Stage 3 still find it hard to accept that humans are animals. This leads to difficulties appreciating that organs (for example in a dog) perform the same function as those in a human. They tend to hold the belief that there are three main classes of living organisms – plants, animals and humans. Comparing and contrasting the features of each can help them to accept that humans are animals.

Misconception: Organisms are either animals or plants. At Key Stage 2 many pupils are taught that living organisms fall into two groups – the Plant and Animal Kingdoms. This may lead to the misconception that there are only two kingdoms.

At Key Stage 3, pupils need to be aware that there are other organisms such as algae, bacteria and fungi that need three additional kingdoms – protoctists, prokaryotes and fungi – to accommodate them. This idea will be explained further in *chapter 11: variation and classification*.

Misconception: Blood can't be a tissue. Few pupils will realise that blood is an example of a tissue. The cells are not joined together and are not similar in appearance. However, it can behave as a group of cells working together with a specific function – a tissue.

For example, when a person cuts themselves:

· white blood cells fight infection
· platelets (cell fragments) help form a network of fibres
· red blood cells are trapped in the fibres
· a blood clot is created
· the blood clot hardens to form a scab.

Found in blood (a tissue). From left to right: red blood cell, white blood cell, platelet

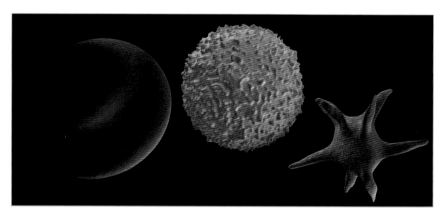

Misconception: Skin is a tissue, not an organ. Many pupils believe the liver or the brain is the largest organ. In fact it is the skin.

Pupils often classify the skin as a tissue, not an organ. They see it as a thin layer covering the surface of the body. The skin contains blood vessels, nerve cells, sweat glands, hair follicles and fat tissue. For an average adult, the skin has a surface area of between 1.5 – 2.0 m², and accounts for around 15% of a person's body mass.

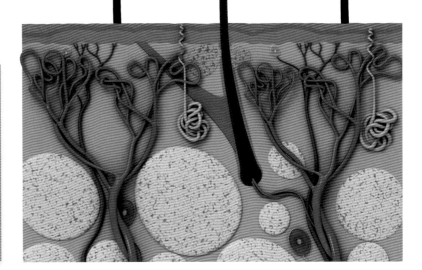

> *Show pupils an unlabelled diagram of a section through the skin. Use directed questioning and their knowledge of the skin and its functions to elicit suggestions for labels of the structures. They should be able to recognise that skin is an organ, as it contains a number of different tissues working together.*

history and culture

Alcmaeon, a Greek living in the fifth century BC, was the first known person to work scientifically by dissecting corpses for anatomical research. He was trying to find the location of human intelligence. Since a blow to the head can affect the mind, he deduced that the head must be the seat of intelligence. Subsequent Greek philosophers (including Aristotle) ignored his conclusions and decided that reasoning came from the heart.

The gladiators' physician

In the third century BC, Herophilus and Erasistratus dissected living criminals. The most influential anatomical researcher of ancient times was another Greek, Galen. In 158 AD he was appointed as chief physician to the gladiators of Pergamum. From the study of wounds and the dissection of pigs and apes, he was able to write hundreds of medical tracts on body organs. He dispelled many erroneous ideas held for centuries, such as the then 600-year-old belief that arteries contained air and carried it around the body from the lungs (the arteries of dead animals appear empty).

Galen himself made many false assumptions, since he believed that the animals he dissected had the same structure as humans. The lack of scientific activity through the middle ages meant that, in Europe, further advances in anatomical knowledge were not made for over a thousand years. From about 1489, Leonardo da Vinci dissected around thirty human corpses, until Pope Leo X forced him to stop. He made many detailed drawings, of which around 750 still exist today, but the teachings of Galen still held sway.

Galen

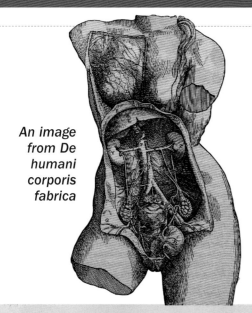

An image from De humani corporis fabrica

Sixteenth century physicians taught human anatomy using Galen's texts, followed by dissections of animals by barber-surgeons. Vesalius, however, decided to carry out his own dissections and demonstrated that Galen's observations were accurate for the apes he had dissected, but not for humans. Using the latest technology in 1543, at the age of only thirty, he revolutionised the science of anatomy by publishing seven volumes of brilliant woodcut illustrations (*De humani corporis fabrica*).

For many hundreds of years the works of Aristotle, Galen and Arab authors had been considered to be unassailable truth and no-one had dared to questioned them. Vesalius made a gigantic break from mediaeval practice by adopting scientific hands-on observation as a direct test of the evidence.

hot topics

*Ask pupils to research aspects of organ donation for a class discussion. Example questions could be: 'Will you donate your organs after you die?'; 'Should the law be changed so you have to say when you **don't** want your organs donated?'*

Ask them to find facts to justify their decisions.

Pupils can find useful information about organ transplants and donations on the UK transplant website.

Organ donation

An organ transplant involves moving a whole or partial organ from one body to another, to replace one that is damaged or failing.

Organs which have been successfully transplanted include the heart, kidneys, liver and lungs. Successful transplants can have a miraculous effect on recipients, allowing many to lead a full and healthy life.

Nearly 3000 people in the UK benefit from organ donation each year.

Automatic organ donation

Currently, thousands of people worldwide are waiting on transplant lists. In the meantime they often have to undergo intense and unpleasant treatment. Unfortunately, many die before a suitable immunologically compatible organ becomes available.

In the UK, most transplanted organs are voluntarily donated after the death, although kidneys and some tissues can be donated by living donors. In some countries, organs may be legally removed after death unless dissent has previously been indicated. This has been suggested as a way to end the current shortage of transplant organs in the UK.

Ethics

This topic should be dealt with sensitively. Discussion of organ transplantation may be distressing to some pupils, particularly those who have friends or relatives involved in the process.

Some religious beliefs ban transplants.

The arguments for and against transplant should be put forward from a neutral position.

Xenografts and xenotransplantation

Transplant of animal tissues or organs is one method used to tackle the shortage of donors. Pigs are often used because of the similarity of their tissues to humans. For example, pig heart valve transplants are successful and common. In the future, genetic modification may be used to make rejection of transplants from other species to humans less likely.

Growing organs

Science fact or science fiction?

This famous image shows research by Charles Vacanti. How was the mouse produced? This poses an excellent basis for discussion. Most pupils believe it had been genetically engineered to grow a human ear.

In fact, a human ear-shaped mould of biodegradable fibres was coated with cartilage cells from a cow. This was then implanted into a hairless (nude) mouse. The mouse's blood enabled the cells to grow, eventually replacing the mould with cartilage. Techniques like this could be used to grow ears and noses for use in plastic surgery.

Scientists have grown skin in the laboratory which can be used for grafts to replace tissue damaged by burns. They have also grown tendons, cartilage, bladders and, most recently, heart valves. None of these structures have the complexity of organs, but in the future it may be possible for scientists to grow organs for transplantation, replacing the need for donors.

Literacy activity

In some cases, How Science Works involves ethical issues and opinions based on scientific knowledge.

Ask pupils how they feel about growing human tissue and organs by using animals. When do they think it is morally acceptable, if ever, to use animals for medical research? Pupils could answer a question through a piece of extended writing, using scientific facts to explain their views.

It is important to be aware of the sensitive nature of these issues and to take account of the feelings of individuals. It is advisable to 'test the water' before proceeding.

facts and figures

Ten amazing body facts to wow your pupils ...

1. Your brain contains about 100 billion nerve cells.
2. Your nerve impulses can travel to your brain at up to 170 mph.
3. Every two weeks your stomach produces a new layer of mucus – otherwise it would digest itself.
4. Your eyes are the same size they were at birth, but your nose and ears never stop growing.
5. 15 million blood cells are destroyed and replaced in your body every second.
6. Your heart creates enough pressure to squirt blood nine metres.
7. You spent about half an hour of your life as a single cell.
8. You shed and regrow your outer skin cells every 27 days (that's nearly 1000 new skins in a lifetime).
9. Your skin weighs about six times as much as your brain.
10. In 24 hours, you breathe about 23 000 times.

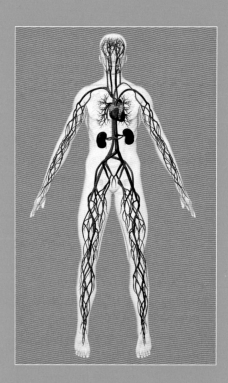

the journey so far

During Key Stage 2, pupils should have learnt

- to locate their heart in their body
- that the heart is protected by the ribs
- to describe simply the function of the heart as a muscle that pumps regularly
- that blood flows around their body in blood vessels
- that if they cut themselves blood flows out of their body
- that the blood forms a scab to stop blood loss and mend the cut
- when harmful micro-organisms (sometimes called germs) enter the body, they can cause disease.

They may have seen a model of the heart and be aware of variation in thickness of the walls. However, at Key Stage 2 they do not need to consider the detailed structure and function of the heart. Most pupils are likely to have used the terms artery and vein, but at this stage they do not need to know that there are different types of blood vessel.

the science at key stage 3

The circulatory (cardiovascular) system carries substances around the body. Materials that are needed are taken to cells. Waste substances are removed. The emphasis at Key Stage 3 should be on this transport function of the blood and the need for the efficient action of the heart to maintain health.

The system is made up of the heart and blood vessels – the arteries, capillaries and veins. They carry the blood around the body. This process is called circulation.

The Heart

The heart is a muscle which constantly pumps blood to all parts of the body. The blood delivers oxygen and nutrients to cells and removes waste.

The heart contains four chambers. The ventricles are at the bottom and the atria at the top. These form two pumps attached side by side to give separate lung and body circulations. The right pump collects blood from the body and pumps this blood to the lungs to collect oxygen. The left pump collects the blood from the lungs. It has a thicker walled ventricle with more muscle to pump blood to the rest of the body at very high pressure. Each pump contains valves to stop the blood from flowing backwards.

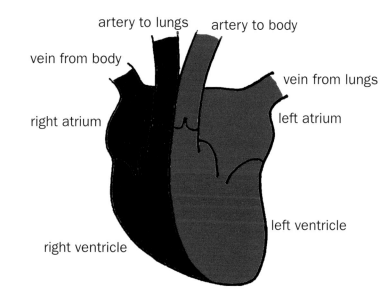

Blood

Blood is made up of:

- red blood cells – carry oxygen
- plasma – straw coloured liquid which is mainly water but contains digested food, waste (for example, carbon dioxide and urea), hormones, blood cells and antibodies
- white blood cells – fight disease by engulfing microbes and making antibodies
- platelets – fragments of cells which help the blood to clot.

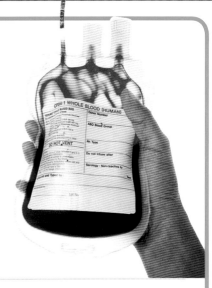

Blood vessels

Blood travels around the body in blood vessels. There are three types of blood vessel.

arteries	veins	capillaries
Carry oxygen-rich blood away from the heart under high pressure.	Carry blood low in oxygen back to the heart at low pressure.	Are very tiny vessels.
Have thick, elastic walls to withstand the high pressure.	Have thin walls.	Have a wall which is only one cell thick, so substances can move through them easily.
The walls stretch with each heart beat to give a pulse as the blood flows along.	Contain valves to stop blood flowing backwards.	Every cell in the body is close to a capillary.

the journey ahead

During Key Stage 4, pupils will learn about the circulatory and immune systems in greater detail. They will study:

- the detailed structure of the heart including its pattern of contraction and relaxation and the body's double circulatory system
- the structure of blood vessels, and become familiar with the use of the terms oxygenated and deoxygenated blood
- how blood cells function - the role of haemoglobin in carrying oxygen, how white blood cells prevent disease, and the role of platelets in scab formation (this is first introduced in this book in *chapter 10: staying healthy*)
- the differences between bacteria and viruses, and the mechanisms by which they cause disease in the body (this is first introduced in this book in *chapter 9: micro-organisms*).

teaching issues

> **Circulatory anagrams**
>
> *Place a few anagrams of key words such as platelet, artery and capillary on the board for pupils to unscramble while you take the register. More frequent use will help them to remember them and to spell them correctly.*

Vocabulary and use of language

Common use of anatomical terms

There are a lot of new terms used in this topic. Many pupils will have heard them used before, as they are regularly referred to in everyday situations. For example, anti-smoking adverts often show the link between smoking and the narrowing and hardening of arteries. Draw out misconceptions by asking pupils what they think common terms may mean, before giving them the answer.

Oxygenated and deoxygenated blood

The terms oxygenated and deoxygenated do not have to be used at this level. However, they are useful descriptive terms which aid pupils understanding of what the blood is doing at a particular time. Explain the use of the prefix 'de', meaning to remove. For example, de-icer is used to remove ice from a car windscreen.

Veins and arteries

Many pupils find it difficult to remember the difference between veins and arteries. Try teaching them the following hints to aid their memory. The words artery and away begin with an 'a' – arteries take blood away from the heart. The word vein contains the word 'in' – veins take blood back into the heart.

Emphasise these differences by relating them to the differences in the pressure of blood and the associated thicknesses of the walls of the vessels. Although not essential, it is useful at this stage to establish that arteries carry blood under high pressure away from the heart, including to the lungs, so that the fallacy that all arteries carry oxygenated blood can be avoided.

Valves

Pupils often have difficulty understanding how valves in the heart and veins operate; they think they open and close themselves. Use simple diagrams or animations to show how valves ensure one-way flow by being opened or closed by movement of blood.

Misconceptions

Misconception: The heart is in the left-hand side of the chest. Pupils will have an idea of where they think their heart is. The heart is located in the chest between the lungs, behind the sternum and above the diaphragm. The centre of the heart is located only a couple of centimetres off the centre of the body (midsagittal plane). However, the heart is tipped, so more of the muscle is located in the left-hand side of the chest. Approximately two thirds of the heart lies to the left of the midline of the body.

Misconception: The heart is 'heart-shaped'. The heart does indeed form a slight tip at the bottom, but it is not as pronounced as in a cartoon depiction. Also, there are not two curved regions at the top. Showing the pupils a photograph of the human heart or, better still, carrying out a dissection of an animal heart, will enable pupils to address this misconception.

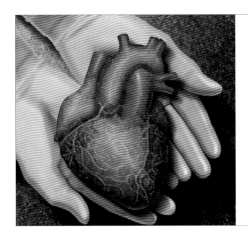 

The human heart is not actually 'heart-shaped'.

Misconception: Anatomical diagrams are 'mirror images'. Pupils get very confused when they are labelling the left- and right-hand sides of the heart. Many find it hard to understand why the left side of the heart in a diagram is on their right hand side. If they face someone else, they will see that their own right hand is opposite the other person's left. A dissection of the body would be drawn with the left-hand side of the heart on the right-hand side of the paper.

Pupils could stick a paper copy of a heart onto their jumper and label the left-hand and right-hand side. If they remove the piece of paper and stick it in their notes, they will realise that the right-hand side of their heart actually appears on the left-hand side of the page.

Misconception: Blood without oxygen is blue. This is untrue. All human blood, and the blood of other organisms which use haemoglobin, is red. However, the shade varies depending on the amount of oxygen that is present. If blood is fully oxygenated, it appears bright red. If it is deoxygenated, it appears dark red. This can be seen when venous blood (blood taken from a vein) is taken for testing, or blood is donated.

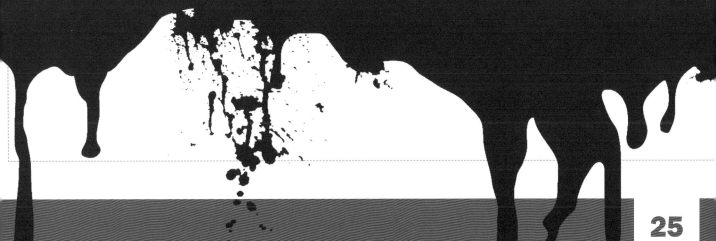

The fallacy may arise because veins near the surface of the skin appear blue. This is caused by a number of factors, involving the absorption and scattering of different wavelengths of light as they pass in and out of the skin and are reflected from the veins. There is also a contrast effect between the emitted wavelengths from the veins and the neighbouring skin, which affects visual perception.

Show pupils a photograph of someone having a blood specimen taken from their vein to help dismiss the misconception that blood in veins is blue.

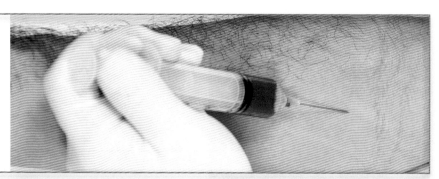

The misconception that venous blood is blue is compounded by the conventional colour-coding in text books of red for arteries (or for oxygenated blood) and blue for veins (or for deoxygenated blood).

Pupils will have to become used to these diagrams as their study of science continues. At this stage, however, draw diagrams using a colour coding system of bright red (oxygenated blood) and dark red (deoxygenated blood) to help pupils get it right.

lungs

rest of body

Misconception: The heart pumps blood all the way around the body. Pupils do not need to know that the heart pumps blood only as far as the capillaries, where other mechanisms take over. However, to aid later learning it is probably better to avoid the phrase 'pumps blood around the body', for example by describing the action of the heart as 'pumping blood to the tissues'. From here the blood flows back to the heart (but not through the pumping action of the heart).

Some pupils believe that the blood only flows to certain parts of the body. Help them overcome this misconception by emphasising the transport functions of the blood and the need for all living cells to receive and remove materials.

applications and implications

Science at home

Fitness levels can be monitored by studying pulse rate. Many people take their pulse at home (resting pulse rate) and while they are exercising (exercising pulse rate) using their fingers or an automated machine. Resting pulse rate usually rises with age and is generally lower in physically fit people. Exercising pulse rate is higher than a resting pulse rate, as the heart has to work harder to pump more oxygenated blood to working muscles.

If regular exercise is maintained, a person's heart rate will not rise as high as it once did with the same amount of effort. As a person becomes fitter, the rate will decrease because their heart and lungs have become stronger, the heart stroke volume is higher and gas exchange is more efficient. Many people training for a sport, such as running a marathon, will use measurement of pulse rate to help them plan training programmes.

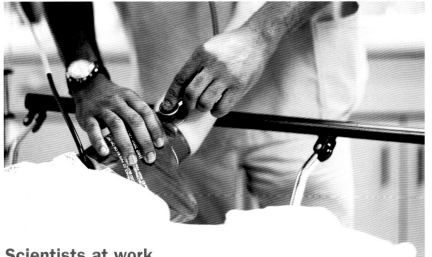

Scientists at work

Vital signs are measurements of the body's most basic functions. They are useful in detecting medical problems. They are regularly monitored by doctors, nurses and paramedics.

There are four main vital signs:

- body temperature
- pulse rate
- respiration rate
- blood pressure.

hot topics

Literacy activity

Arrange for pupils to carry out research on blood donation. Ask them to design a leaflet, to be displayed at local doctors' surgeries, to promote 'giving blood'.

Blood donation

Blood donations save thousands of lives every year. Each donation is normally divided into several components as each part has different medical uses. Therefore, one donation can benefit more than one person. For example,

- red blood cells are used to 'top-up' blood after surgery or accidents
- platelets are given to patients who have been treated for cancer with chemotherapy
- plasma is given to women who have lost blood during childbirth.

Approximately 6% of the population who could give blood actually do so. As blood can only be stored for short periods, it is essential to maintain a regular supply from donors. There is a recurrent shortage and a constant drive to recruit donors.

There is useful information on the National Blood Service website.

history and culture

William Harvey

The Chinese and Arab worlds knew about the circulation of the blood long before it was understood in Europe. William Harvey, an English physician, is credited with being the first westerner to describe blood circulation in detail, based on careful observations and controlled experiments including vivisections of animals. Hieronymous Fabricius, Harvey's tutor in Padua, had discovered valves in veins. Harvey started his research because he was not satisfied with Fabricius' explanation of their function. He noticed that blood could not be pushed down a vein in the arm and other parts of the body – only upwards. The neck was an exception; showing in each case blood in veins was flowing towards the heart.

He decided that blood flowed in a closed system in two loops, one to the lungs and the other to the other parts of the body. He also determined that blood flow was caused by the pumping action of the heart, rather than due to the sucking mechanism that was the theory of the day.

The accepted model of the time went all the way back to Galen in the second century, who believed venous blood and arterial blood to be separate. They were thought to be produced in the liver and heart respectively, from where they flowed to the body tissues to be absorbed.

By the use of experimental and quantitative techniques, Harvey overthrew the old beliefs of the heart as a mystical site of the spirit. He showed that it could be scientifically analysed as a pump.

It was not until later, when Marcello Malpighi used a microscope to discover capillaries, that the connection between arteries and veins was established. Despite being an Italian, Malpighi published most of his research in the journal of the Royal Society of England. In 1661, his first article was about the anatomy of the lung of a frog.

For many centuries China was isolated from the West and Middle East. Much knowledge first discovered by the Chinese, including determining the circulation of the blood, remained unknown to the rest of the world. Similarly, the Indian Atreya is credited with describing the circulation of blood around 400 BC. The Arab Muslim scholar Ibn al-Nafis (born in 1213) also described pulmonary and coronary circulation long before Harvey. He was considered to be the greatest physiologist of the middle ages, but his works remained in obscurity in Europe.

The sixteenth century Spaniard, Michael Servetus, was the first European to describe pulmonary circulation in a theological work, 'Christianismi Restitutio'. Most of the copies were burned soon after publication. Soon after, Servatus himself was burned at the stake with what was thought to be the last copy of his book chained to his leg. Three surviving copies remained hidden for decades.

Harvey's work was important because it provided convincing scientific evidence and, despite much original opposition, became widely accepted in his lifetime.

Literacy task

Provide pupils with sources to research the historical work of early investigators such as Galen, Ibn al-Nafis, Vesalius and Harvey. Set teams the task of researching and reporting on the work and ideas of each historical figure. Discuss why ideas were held for long periods and how and why eventually they were challenged and changed. The international nature of science and the importance of good evidence and effective communication will become apparent. Simple accounts of scientific historical figures can be found on the timelinescience website.

facts and figures

Answers to common questions posed by pupils:

· Your heart is about the size of your fist.
· A woman's heart has a mass of approximately 250g and a man's 300g.
· Your heart beats approximately 100 000 times a day – that's over 2.5 billion times in a 70 year lifetime.
· Your heart pumps about 10 000 dm³ (litres) of blood a day.
· It takes about 20 seconds for a blood cell to pass completely round the double circulation.
· Women have approximately 4.5 dm³ (litres) of blood in their body, men have around 1 dm³ more.
· If all your blood vessels (including capillaries) were laid out end to end, they would stretch over twice around the world – that's more than 60 000 miles.

Literacy task

Challenge pupils to find and record their 'most interesting fact' about the heart and circulation. They will find out a lot more in the process! Collate and share the findings with the class.

the journey so far

During Key Stage 2, pupils should have learnt:

- the functions of incisor, canine and molar teeth
- herbivores and carnivores have different types of teeth to suit their diet
- tooth decay is caused by bacteria in the mouth producing acid, and mechanisms for preventing tooth decay, such as brushing regularly
- humans and other animals need food for activity and growth
- that to stay healthy, you must eat a balanced diet
- the four main food groups are carbohydrates, fats, proteins and vitamins and minerals, the role in the body of each and an example of a source of each.

the science at key stage 3

To remain healthy, a person must eat a balanced diet. Ingested food enters the digestive system where it is broken down using mechanical and chemical processes. Digested foods are absorbed by the body and used for growth and repair. Undigested waste is egested from the body.

Balanced diet

For a balanced diet, a person must consume each of the seven food groups in the correct quantities. Nutrient deficiencies cause poor health – too little fibre causes constipation and insufficient iron leads to anaemia, for example. The amount of each nutrient required varies dramatically: an average adult needs about 65 g of fat per day compared with only 60 mg of vitamin C.

food group	main roles in the body	examples of food
carbohydrates	provide energy (used in respiration)	pasta, potatoes, bread
proteins	growth and repair	fish, meat, eggs
fats	store of energy, insulates the body to retain heat and protects vital organs from damage	butter, cheese, oil, meat, nuts
vitamins	maintain health – insufficient amounts lead to deficiency diseases	fruit, vegetables, fortified cereals, liver, milk, cheese, oily fish
minerals	maintain health – insufficient amounts lead to deficiency diseases	milk (calcium), fish (iodine), red meat (iron)
fibre	adds bulk to food so that waste can be pushed more easily out of the digestive system	cereals, vegetables, fruit
water	cells and body fluids are mainly water; all cell reactions take place in water; it is lost in sweat, urine and breathing, so needs constant replacement	all drinks, most foods

Digestion

Mechanical digestion involves the use of the teeth to chew, tear and grind food into smaller pieces. Chemical digestion uses enzymes to break large food molecules into smaller molecules which can then be absorbed. Water, vitamins and minerals are small enough to be absorbed without digestion (more details are given in the section *teaching issues*. Fibre cannot be digested.

The digestive system

When eating, the food begins the following journey:

 Mouth: Carbohydrate digestion starts.

 Oesophagus (gullet): Food pushed to stomach.

 Stomach: Protein digestion starts. Strong hydrochloric acid kills most micro-organisms.

 Pancreas: secretes digestive enzymes into the small intestine

Small intestine: Carbohydrates, proteins and fats digested. Soluble food is absorbed into blood stream through villi which produce a large surface area for absorption.

 Liver: secretes bile into the small intestine where it helps to digest fats

 Large intestine: Most of the remaining water is absorbed

 Rectum: Stores faeces (undigested remains).

 Anus: Faeces pass out of the body.

the journey ahead

During Key Stage 4, pupils will learn about the digestive system in much greater detail. They will study:

- the detailed structure of a villus, and how substances are absorbed into the bloodstream
- the structure and function of enzymes
- how enzyme action is affected by variables such as temperature and pH
- the use of enzymes in industrial processes, such as in the manufacture of baby foods and in biological detergents.

teaching issues

Collecting food labels

Have pupils collect food labels and challenge them to explain the traffic light system and/or GDAs. Spirited debate should ensue. Have a good collection of your own labels handy to supplement theirs.

Breaking molecules

Use simple models and schematic diagrams to show how big molecules can be built up or broken down. Use different shapes to show the various 'building blocks', for example hexagons for sugars, circles for amino acids and rectangles for glycerol and fatty acids.

Recognising enzymes

After looking at the names of the three main types of enzyme (carboyhdrase, lipase and protease) ask pupils:

"What tells you that they are enzymes?" Suggest that 'ase' is rather like a surname – these molecules belong to the enzyme family.

"How can you recognise what they do?" The link to carbohydrates and proteins is easy; explain that lipid is the scientific name for fats and oils.

Vocabulary and use of language

A great many new and unfamiliar terms and concepts are introduced in this topic. It is very difficult to take it all on board if all aspects are covered at once. Pupils should be introduced to the topic gradually and given the chance to rehearse new words and ideas before moving on.

Possible teaching sequence

Learning the new terms can be assisted by considering self-contained topics which build up in a logical sequence such as this:

1. Food types – the seven foods needed in the diet and their uses in the body
2. Nutrition – the major sources of the different food types, the concepts of a balanced diet and healthy eating
3. Big molecules – carbohydrates, fats and proteins and why they cannot be absorbed
4. Digestion – how big molecules are broken down
5. Enzymes – biological catalysts: carbohydrases, lipase and proteases and their actions
6. The major organs and layout of the gut
7. Digestion in the gut – the role of each organ
8. Absorption – the need for a thin lining, a large surface area and a transport system
9. Water absorption and egestion – the formation and removal of faeces

Naming of enzymes

Three main types of enzymes break down large, insoluble molecules into small, soluble molecules which can be absorbed into the blood:

1. Carbohydrases break down starch into sugars.
2. Proteases break down proteins into amino acids.
3. Lipases breakdown fats into fatty acids and glycerol.

An enzyme is normally named after the substrate or the chemical reaction it catalyses. The suffix –ase is added to the end of the name, denoting that it is an enzyme.

The name of the protein DNA polymerase:

it acts on DNA   it is an enzyme

DNA polymerase

it catalyses polymerisation

Confusing sugars and enzymes

Later, pupils may confuse sugars and enzymes such as sucrose and sucrase, lactose and lactase. Introduce them to the idea that sugars end in -ose now to help to avoid this confusion later.

Egestion and excretion

Pupils often confuse the terms egestion and excretion. They both mean getting rid of waste but they refer to different types of waste:

Egestion is the removal of undigested food from the body. Solid wastes (faeces) are removed during egestion.

Excretion is the removal of waste produced by chemical reactions in the body. Excreted wastes are in liquids and gases. They include urea in urine and sweat, and carbon dioxide in exhaled air.

Misconceptions

Misconception: Enzymes are living things. Many pupils believe that enzymes are living things – tiny organisms which swim about the cell chopping up food. They may talk about enzymes being 'killed'. Enzymes are actually proteins produced by cells to speed up a specific chemical reaction. Emphasise that enzymes are molecules and that as proteins they can be large with complex, precise shapes (see following section).

Misconception: Enzymes look like a pair of scissors. Many teachers use the analogy that enzymes are like scissors, chopping up a long molecule into small pieces. However, each type of enzyme has a unique 3D shape. Within the shape there is an active site, where the substrate binds to the enzyme. Therefore, this is where the chemical reaction takes place. A substrate is the substance the enzyme acts on.

Misconception: Enzymes are used up. Often pupils say that, once an enzyme has been used to speed up a reaction, it cannot be used again. Enzymes are biological catalysts – they speed up a reaction without being used up.

Misconception: Enzymes are only found in the gut. Common misconceptions include believing that enzymes are only used for digestion and only found in digestive secretions. Enzymes control chemical reactions inside all cells.

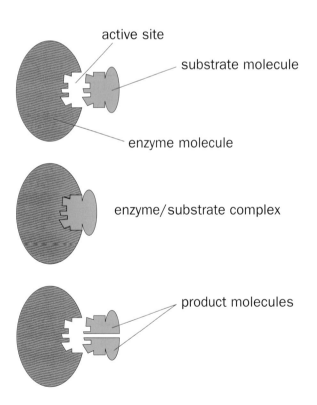

Once an enzyme has finished catalysing one reaction it is ready to catalyse the next.

Enzymes inside cells

When introducing chemical digestion and the use of enzymes to catalyse the breakdown of foods, challenge pupils to think of other chemical reactions that go on in the body. Ask them what will happen to the digested food. Explain that enzymes are used to release energy by breaking down molecules in respiration and to build up proteins, to make cell structures.

Misconception: Enzymes only break things down. Another common misconception is that enzymes only break down molecules. Enzymes can perform one of three functions:

1. Break down large molecules.
2. Build up large molecules from small ones.
3. Turn one molecule into another one.

Try to establish the ubiquitous nature of enzymes inside cells and their roles in anabolic as well as catabolic reactions by discussing roles other than digestion, when introducing their use in the gut.

Misconception: Digestion begins in the stomach. Many pupils hold the belief that chemical digestion begins in the stomach. It usually begins in the mouth: the salivary glands secrete amylase which breaks down starch into maltose.

This can be demonstrated by asking pupils to chew a piece of bread for an extended period of time. The bread begins to taste sweet as the starches are digested.

Some individuals do not secrete salivary amylase. This does not affect digestion of starch, since pancreatic amylase completes the job.

Misconception: GDAs tell you how much you should eat. The guideline daily amounts (GDAs) found on food labels do not tell you how much of each foodstuff you need to consume every day. They are merely a *guide* for making appropriate dietary choices – the values are approximate benchmarks. They cannot be used as individual targets for a healthy diet, because:

· individuals vary (size, gender, activity levels, age and health, etc.)
· GDAs for children are provided for food targeted at children
· GDAs are usually for a 'typical adult', usually the data for an average woman (to discourage over-consumption)
· GDAs can vary according to the system being used
· it is almost impossible to consume the correct mix of foods to get the GDAs for all nutrients in a single day.

GUIDELINE DAILY AMOUNTS		
	women	men
energy	2000 calories	2500 calories
protein	45 g	55 g
carbohydrate	230 g	300 g
of which sugars	90 g	120 g
fat	70 g	95 g
of which saturates	20 g	30 g
fibre	24 g	24 g
sodium	2.4 g	2.4 g
equivalent as salt	6 g	6 g

Science at home

Indigestion tablets

In the stomach, food is mixed with hydrochloric acid. It has a pH of about 2. The acid has two key roles:

1. It kills any micro-organsims present in the food, preventing them causing disease.

2. It provides optimum conditions for the protease enzyme, pepsin, to digest proteins.

Food is sealed in your stomach by two strong circular muscles – the oesophageal sphincter at the top and pyloric sphincter at the base.

Indigestion (heartburn) occurs when stomach acid comes into contact with the sensitive, protective lining (mucosa) of the digestive system. The acid breaks down the mucosa, causing irritation and inflammation. One of the main causes of recurring indigestion is acid reflux. This occurs when the oesophageal sphincter fails to prevent stomach acid from coming back up into your oesophagus.

Indigestion tablets contain alkaline substances such as calcium carbonate which react with and neutralise hydrochloric acid. These help to decrease the acidity of excess stomach acid, relieving the pain and symptoms of indigestion.

Antacid tablets are used by people to relieve the symptoms of indigestion.

Biological detergents

A biological detergent is a washing powder which contains enzymes. Lipases and proteases are used to break down fat and protein molecules present in biological stains, such as food and blood, on clothes. The soluble fatty acids, glycerol and amino acids produced are then removed during the washing process. The use of enzymes in detergents means that effective washing can be carried out at lower temperatures. Advantages of enzyme use are:

- lower energy consumption
- coloured clothing maintains its intensity as the dye is less likely to wash out of the fabric
- clothes are more likely to maintain their shape - hot water can cause fabric to shrink
- only a very small quantity of enzymes is required to replace large quantities of man-made chemicals.

Although biological detergents have many advantages, some people are allergic to specific enzymes. This can cause skin problems, such as eczema. Non-biological detergents are recommended for washing baby clothes.

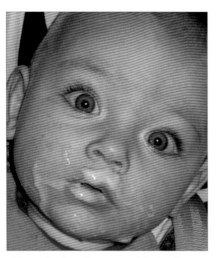

Trypsin is often used in baby food. This makes it easier for a baby to digest the food.

Scientists at work

For thousands of years, enzymes have been used to make various food and drink products. These include cheese, yoghurt, bread, beer and wine. Enzymes also play a huge role in the manufacture of new products in the biotechnology industries.

Creation of fructose syrup for slimming products

Isomerase converts glucose syrup into much sweeter fructose syrup. A small amount of fructose can replace a larger amount of glucose in a food, without a loss of sweetness. This technique is used in preparing foods which are aimed at assisting people to lose weight. The less sugar present, the lower the energy content.

Manufacture of baby foods

Proteases (normally trypsin) are often used in the manufacture of baby food. Protein molecules are partly broken down into amino acids, making it easier for babies to digest the food.

hot topics

Food poisoning activity

Challenge pupils to come up with as many mechanisms as possible for preventing food poisoning, such as maintaining good personal hygiene, thorough cooking and prevention of cross contamination (for example, contact of raw meat or contaminated utensils with cooked food).

They could use their answers to draw rules to be followed in a professional kitchen.

Food Poisoning

Food poisoning is caused by eating food contaminated with bacteria or toxins. Bacteria can rapidly multiply from one to millions under favourable conditions of moisture, food and warmth. The more bacteria present, the higher the chance of infection and illness.

Symptoms include diarrhoea, vomiting, and stomach cramps. They normally begin 4–36 hours after eating contaminated food.

Three types of bacteria are responsible for most cases of food poisoning – *Salmonella*, *E. coli* and *Campylobacter*.

Christmas turkeys

Most poultry is contaminated with *Salmonella*. Thorough cooking completely kills the bacteria and no toxins remain to cause problems. However, underthawing of frozen turkeys is a major cause of food poisoning. Large birds in particular take many hours to thaw completely, even though they appear defrosted on the surface. Cooking just warms up the deeper meat enough to encourage rapid growth of the bacteria.

The body's response

The acid in your stomach will destroy most micro-organsims present in food and drink. Unfortunately, food poisoning bacteria are resistant. If there are large numbers, the immune system will become involved. Micro-organisms may be destroyed by white blood cells, or during a fever. The body may also remove many of the micro-organisms in the body by vomiting or through diarrhoea. This will decrease the number it has to fight off.

In most cases, a person will recover naturally in a couple of days. Consequently, most cases of food poisoning are not reported and the total number of cases is unknown. However, with severe food poisoning, a person may require hospital treatment.

Oral rehydration therapy

Dehydration caused by food poisoning is a major cause of death in babies and young children in undeveloped countries. Food poisoning bacteria like *Salmonella* bacteria release endotoxins when they die. These irritate the gut lining, increase the rate of movement through the gut and block the normal water uptake channels, causing diarrhoea.

Effective treatment is simple and very cheap. Oral rehydration therapy (ORT) involves adding a little glucose and salt to clean water. It is based on the scientific understanding of the water uptake mechanism of the gut. A co-transport coupling mechanism not affected by food poisoning bacteria comes into play. Glucose molecules are absorbed through the intestinal wall taking sodium ions with them. The uptake of the sodium ions causes water to follow by osmosis. More refined mixtures include potassium ions and sodium hydrogencarbonate to treat the potassium depletion and metabolic acidosis caused by diarrhoea.

The Rehydration Project website gives more detailed information.

Undercooked food on a barbecue is a common source of food poisoning.

> **Diarrhoea and dehydration**
>
> *Diarrhoea can cause rapid dehydration. We absorb over 10 dm^3 of water through the gut lining every day. Just over one fifth of this comes from food and drink, the rest is about 8 dm^3 from the digestive juices we secrete.*

> *UNICEF/WHO oral rehydration salts (ORS) per dm^3 of boiled water:*
>
> *sodium chloride 3.5 g*
>
> *sodium hydrogencarbonate 2.5 g*
>
> *potassium chloride 1.5 g*
>
> *glucose 20 g*

facts and figures

Diet is one of the most important factors affecting health in the UK today yet, because of its complexity, providing useful data that people can act on is extremely difficult.

Health facts

In the UK:

- the current trend of unhealthy eating and lifestyle is likely to lead to one in four people in the UK becoming obese by 2010
- poor diet and unhealthy lifestyle cause more than 200 000 people to die prematurely every year due to coronary heart disease, stroke and other illnesses

- more than 80% of men, and nearly 70% of women, eat too much salt; most are unaware because about 75% of the salt is already in the food we buy.

Eating a healthier diet could help protect against cancers, diabetes, osteoporosis, heart disease, strokes and tooth decay along with many other diet-related conditions.

Nutrition education

The European Food Information Council (EUFIC), Food Standards Agency (FSA) and BBC Health/Nutrition websites contain useful information. The British Nutrition Foundation website includes useful teaching resources.

FSA Eatwell plate

Problems faced in trying to improve eating habits in the UK are illustrated on the section of the FSA website which explains the change from the *Balance of good health plate* to *The eatwell plate*. Even *The eatwell plate* has come under criticism. East Sussex County Council's Trading Standards team found that the majority of nurseries in the area were providing food that was too low in energy, fat and saturated fat and too high in fruit and vegetables. *The eatwell plate* is only suitable for children over the age of five.

Food labelling

Guidline Daily Amounts (GDAs) for energy intake, fat, saturated fat, carbohydrate, total sugars, protein, fibre, sodium and salt for adults are based on typical requirements for healthy men and women over 18 years of age and of normal weight. For example, the energy GDA values are derived from estimated average requirements (EAR) for energy. They take account of the activity levels and lifestyle of an average person (fairly sedentary). For an average woman and man, the energy GDA is 2000 kcal ('Calories') and 2500 kcal respectively.

Vitamin or mineral content in a food label is given as a percentage of the recommended dietary allowance (RDA) rather than the GDA. Vitamins and minerals are needed in specific amounts for essential metabolic reactions in the body and the maintenance of good health. Therefore, unlike GDAs, recommended levels are set higher than the average requirement in order to eliminate deficiency. The RDA is the average daily intake that will meet the requirement of nearly all healthy adult people. As with GDAs, they represent the average intake over a period of time and not the amounts that should be taken every day.

Gory story

In 1822 French-Canadian trapper Alexis St Martin suffered a shooting accident. It tore away part of his abdominal wall and chest, removing part of a rib and lacerating his stomach and left lung, which both bulged out of the wound. The remains of his breakfast oozed out of a hole in the stomach. Fortunately, the surgeon William Beaumont was at hand: he removed bone fragments, damaged tissue and scraps of clothing and replaced the lung and stomach. Against the odds, St Martin survived. However, the edges of his wound healed to his abdomen wall leaving a hole to the outside. Beaumont conducted a series of experiments, placing food tied to string through the hole and extracting digestive juices for analysis. St Martin survived another fifty eight years. His family let his body rot before they buried him, to dissuade medics who wanted to perform an autopsy from digging him up.

Food poisoning

According to *The Lancet* (2005), almost two-million children die from dehydration caused by diarrhoea, every year.

The importance of oral rehydration therapy

Some say ORT is the most important medical discovery of the twentieth century. In fact, Indian surgeon Sushruta prescribed rice water, coconut juice and carrot juice for the treatment of acute diarrhoea more than 2500 years ago.

Irish physician William O'Shaughnessy found loss of water and salt in the stool of cholera patients. Using hypertonic intravenous solutions, he saved patients on the brink of death. Mortality rate dropped from 70% to 40%. This was in 1831.

Animal experiments in the 1950s established that sodium and glucose were transported together through intestinal epithelium. Oral rehydration therapy was then developed for the treatment of cholera in the late 1960s by researchers in India and Bangladesh.

During the Indo-Pakistani War of 1971 medical teams in the refugee camps ran out of intravenous fluids. ORT reduced the death rate to only 3%, compared with 20–30% using only intravenous fluid therapy.

Today, UNICEF distributes oral rehydration solution sachets to about sixty different developing countries.

For its role in developing Oral Rehydration Solution, The International Centre for Diarrhoeal Disease Research, Bangladesh, received the first *Gates Award for Global Health*. Norbert Hirschhorn, Dilip Mahalanabis, David R. Nalin, and Nathaniel F. Pierce were awarded the first Pollin Prize for Paediatric Research in 2002.

Botulism and botox

Botulinum toxin, a neurotoxin produced by Clostridium botulinum, is possibly the most acutely toxic substance known, with a median lethal dose of 1 ng kg^{-1}. Death is caused by paralysis which spreads downwards from the face until breathing ceases. 'Botulism' (from the Latin botulus, for sausage) was coined by a German doctor, Muller, after another German doctor, Justinus Kerner, described the toxin as 'sausage poison'. Fortunately for sausage eaters and others, botulism food poisoning is rare.

As Botox, the toxin is used in minute doses as a cosmetic treatment to remove wrinkles by paralysing facial muscles.

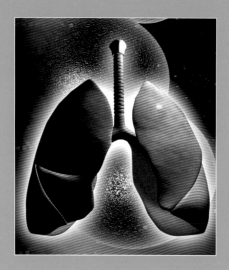

the journey so far

During Key Stage 2, pupils should have learnt:
*   to locate their lungs in their body
*   that you breathe to take in oxygen and remove carbon dioxide
*   that you breathe faster when you exercise

From their knowledge of living processes, they may know that food can act as a source of energy and that energy is released in respiration. They may understand that during exercise, muscles need more oxygen and produce more carbon dioxide. If they have considered the circulatory system in Key Stage 3 (see *chapter 3: the circulatory system*), they should know that blood transports oxygen from the lungs and carbon dioxide is transported to the lungs.

the science at key stage 3

The respiratory system consists of the lungs, the tubes connecting the lungs to the nose and mouth, and structures in the chest which cause air to move in and out of the lungs.

Its purpose is to take in oxygen and remove carbon dioxide from the body. This process involves ventilation and gas exchange.

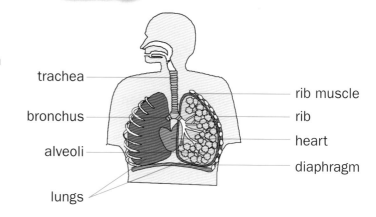

trachea
bronchus
alveoli
lungs
rib muscle
rib
heart
diaphragm

Ventilation

The lungs are located inside the chest cavity (thorax) and are protected by the rib cage. Below the lungs there is a large sheet of muscle called the diaphragm. This separates the thorax from the abdomen. The ribs, rib (intercostal) muscles and diaphragm work together so that air is moved into and out of the lungs. This is called ventilation, or breathing.

Inhaling (breathing in)
*   Rib (intercostal) muscles contract moving the ribcage up and out.
*   Diaphragm contracts and flattens, pressing down on the organs in the abdomen.
*   The volume of the thorax increases.
*   Pressure inside the lungs decreases below the pressure of the air outside, so air is pushed in.

Exhaling (breathing out)

- Intercostal muscles relax and the **ribcage** sinks back.
- **Diaphragm** relaxes and the organs of the abdomen push it back up.
- The volume in the thorax decreases and air is forced out by the contraction of elastic tissue in the lungs.

Note that in normal gentle breathing this is a passive process; muscles (external intercostals and abdominal wall) are only used to force air out when breathing rate is raised.

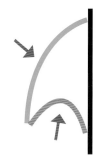

Gas exchange

Alveoli are air sacs which are adapted to allow gas exchange of oxygen and carbon dioxide to happen easily and efficiently. They:

- create a large surface area in the lungs
- have moist, thin walls – only one cell thick
- have a very large blood supply – many capillaries.

During gas exchange, gases move by diffusion from an area of higher concentration to an area of lower concentration. Therefore, oxygen diffuses from the air in the alveoli, into the blood. Carbon dioxide diffuses from the blood, into the air in the alveoli.

Red blood cells carry oxygen from the lungs around the body to all the other living cells. Carbon dioxide is transported in blood plasma from the respiring cells to the lungs, to be removed (a form of excretion).

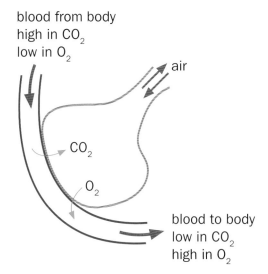

blood from body
high in CO_2
low in O_2

air

CO_2

O_2

blood to body
low in CO_2
high in O_2

Gas exchange in an alveolus.

Respiration

In order to move, grow and stay warm, the body needs energy. Energy is released in cells in the chemical reactions of respiration. The overall process is the same as burning fuels. Respiration can be summarised as:

glucose	+	oxygen	→	carbon dioxide	+	water	energy is given out

$$C_6H_{12}O_6 \quad + \quad 6O_2 \quad \rightarrow \quad 6CO_2 \quad + \quad 6H_2O \qquad \text{energy is given out}$$

In fact, energy is released a little at a time, in many enzyme-controlled small steps.

the journey ahead

During Key Stage 4, pupils learn about the respiratory system in much greater detail. They will study:

- that respiration takes place inside a cell's mitochondria
- the differences between aerobic and anaerobic respiration
- how haemoglobin in red blood cells carries oxygen around the body
- the link between aerobic fitness and exercise (this is first introduced in this book in *chapter 10: staying healthy*)
- diseases of the respiratory system, including emphysema.

teaching issues

Card sorting

Give pupils a pile of cards, each containing the name of one of the main parts of the respiratory system. Ask them to sequence the cards to illustrate the order air would pass through them on its way into/out of the body. Pupils could then annotate each part to explain its function or structure further.

The respiration equation

At Key Stage 3, only the word equation for respiration is required. However, more able pupils find the balanced chemical equation satisfying, as it explains more fully what happens to the reactants. It should also be noted that energy is not a substance. If it is to be included in the respiration equation the term is better placed in brackets.

Vocabulary and use of language

Common use of anatomical terms

There are lots of new anatomical terms used in this topic. Many pupils will have heard some used before in everyday situations. At this level, pupils only need to use the terms windpipe, air sacs and rib muscles. However, many will be able to confidently use the terms trachea, alveoli and intercostal muscles.

Misconceptions

Misconception: Breathing and respiration are the same thing. Pupils commonly believe that the terms breathing and respiration are interchangeable.

- Breathing (also known as ventilation) is the taking in and removal of air from the body.
- Respiration usually means the chemical reaction which takes place inside all cells, causing energy to be released from food.

However, depending on the sources being used, respiration has a physiological definition as well as the biochemical definition of energy release.

Respiration is therefore sometimes used in the context of breathing, as in the phrases external respiration (synonymous with breathing), internal respiration (gas exchange at the level of the tissues) and artificial respiration. The terms cell respiration or tissue respiration are therefore sometimes used to distinguish the process of energy release from the processes of ventilation, gas exchange and the transport of oxygen and carbon dioxide.

To avoid all this confusion, at Key Stage 3 it is safest to use respiration solely in the context of energy release.

Literacy task

Pupils can be set an extended writing task, imagining themselves as an oxygen molecule. They then have to describe their journey through a human body. This would begin from the moment they are breathed in, through the process of respiration, until they are later exhaled as part of a carbon dioxide molecule.

Artificial respiration is administered to a person if they stop breathing. This can be misleading by reinforcing the confusion between breathing and respiration.

Misconception: You only breathe in oxygen. Many pupils believe that you only breathe in oxygen and/or that you only breathe out carbon dioxide. The table below shows the main differences between inhaled and exhaled air (other sources may give slightly different values).

	inhaled air	exhaled air
nitrogen	78%	78%
oxygen	21%	16%
carbon dioxide	0.04%	4%
other gases such as argon	about 1%	about 1%
water vapour	ambient concentration	above ambient concentration
temperature	ambient temperature	above ambient temperature

Pupils also tend to focus on the need for oxygen and neglect the importance of the removal of carbon dioxide. If allowed to accumulate, carbon dioxide becomes toxic by lowering the pH of body fluids and affecting enzyme activity. Changes in carbon dioxide concentration are detected by the body and used to regulate breathing rates.

Ask pupils to predict the differences between inhaled and exhaled air. To prove to pupils that the air they breathe out:

1. contains carbon dioxide – ask them to breathe into limewater. It will turn from clear to cloudy.

2. contains oxygen – blow on a glowing splint. It will glow brighter, or relight.

3. contains less oxygen – compare the length of time a candle burns in exhaled air with normal air or the volume changes when oxygen is absorbed by alkaline pyrogallate.

4. is warmer – ask them to breathe gently on their hands. They will feel warm air.

5. contains water vapour – ask them to breathe on a cold window or mirror. They will see condensation. Test the moisture with cobalt chloride paper.

The warnings on plastic bags to keep them away from children are associated with the dangers of rebreathing the CO_2 in exhaled air.

Thorax models

Models are commonly used to demonstrate how changes in the volume of the thorax cause air to be inhaled or exhaled. This can reinforce the misconception that the lungs are empty sacs. Have pupils build their own models using plastic bottles and balloons; then challenge them to identify the differences between their model and the real system.

Misconception: Lungs are empty sacs. Many pupils believe that their lungs are like balloons – empty sacs ready to be filled with air. In fact, the two adult lungs contain approximately 2500 km of airways and 400 million alveoli with a gas exchange surface area of 70 m². They do, however, expand and contract depending on the volume of the air inside them. This is why the analogy of a balloon is used.

This misconception can be addressed by performing a lung dissection. Allow pupils to touch a sheep's lung (wearing gloves). By trying to squash the lung it will demonstrate to them that there are structures inside the lung. Then slice a small piece off the lung and put it into a beaker of water. It will float. This demonstrates that the structure is full of air and not very dense. The lung can also be attached to a pump and inflated, showing pupils its elasticity and its ability to expand to contain lots of air.

Lung volumes

Have pupils measure out an area of 70 m² in a playing field or playground (to represent alveoli) and show them a 5 dm² container (to represent their lungs). This will help them recognise that their lungs contain a very large number of very small alveoli. The surface area of the container can also be found by covering with graph paper.

Misconception: Lungs fill up half the body. Pupils often have a poor conception of the extent of the lungs inside their body – they imagine them to be much larger than they actually are. Ask them to draw lungs in a body outline. Then ask them to feel the position of their rib cage (through their clothes) and show them an anatomical model or pictures of the thorax and abdomen.

Misconception: Food is burnt in the body. A useful analogy to respiration is that of burning foods in the laboratory. However, this can lead to the misconception that miniature combustion reactions are occurring inside cells in the body. It is important to stress that this is not the case, but that the idea of energy being released through a reaction with oxygen is essentially the same.

Igniting foods, such as a marshallow (and watching it burn), can illustrate that energy is locked up in food.

[Be aware of pupils with nut allergies.]

Questions to develop understanding

Ask pupils:

- *"Why can you 'see' breath on a cold day?"*

  This will challenge the misconception that they only breathe out carbon dioxide.

- *"How can your body release energy from food?"*

  This will challenge the misconception that breathing is the same as respiration.

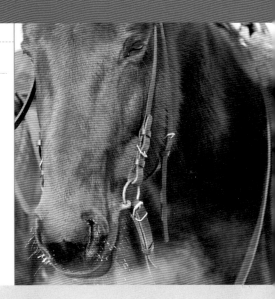

applications and implications

Science at home

Medical terms are used in television programmes like Holby City and Casualty. Encourage pupils to ask about and discuss what they have seen. They might then be asked to explain aspects of programmes to relatives.

Pneumothorax

Pneumothorax is an example of the kind of technical term used by emergency teams and surgeons in television programmes. The thorax is normally air tight, but if the chest cavity is punctured by a broken rib or stabbing, the air can get in and out through the hole instead of the normal airways. The elastic lung collapses and breathing fails to inflate it.

Scientists at work

Paramedics must understand how the respiratory system works and use this knowledge to check for signs of life. If a person has stopped breathing, they may need to administer mouth to mouth resuscitation. This is also known as artificial respiration or 'the kiss of life'.

First aid

Pupils could be encouraged to take part in a first aid course. This will teach procedures like mouth to mouth resuscitation and how to put a person in the recovery position. The Red Cross and St John's Ambulance run a number of courses for young people. You can find information about courses and first aid procedures on their websites.

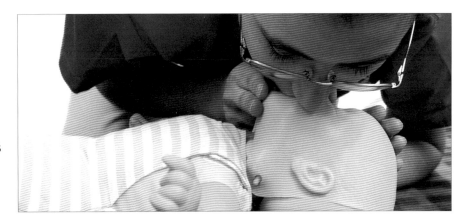

hot topics

Holding your breath

Most people tend to hold their breath naturally a few times each day. It enables you to focus more clearly and concentrate on the task you are performing.

Common situations where a person may hold their breath without knowing include bending to tie a shoelace, or reaching up to take something from a shelf.

Holding your breath for longer

There are several techniques a person can use to improve the length of time they can hold their breath:

1. Slow the heartrate by relaxing and entering a meditative state – reduced heartrate means less oxygen is consumed.
2. Splash cold water on the face – this encourages the heart rate to slow down.
3. Lose weight – it improves the body's efficiency in using oxygen.
4. Take several long deep breaths to flush carbon dioxide from the body. The need to remove carbon dioxide is the most powerful stimulus to force you to breathe.
5. Remain calm – if you start to panic, oxygen is used up more quickly.

Note: Excessive breath holding can be very dangerous.

facts and figures

10 interesting facts on the respiratory system.

These could be used to stimulate discussion work (for example, why is sneezing necessary?)

1. An adult's lungs, on average, can hold about 6 dm³ of air. However, only a small amount of this capacity is used during normal breathing.

2. While resting, a person breathes about 14 to 16 times per minute. After exercise it can increase to more than 60 times per minute.

3. The total surface area of the alveoli in the lungs is approximately equivalent to the size of a tennis court.

4. The lungs are the only organ in the body which can float on water.

5. The lungs produce a detergent-like substance called surfactant. This reduces the surface tension within the alveoli and prevents them from collapsing.

6. While resting, an adult body breathes in and out around 7 dm³ (1.5 gallons) of air each minute.

7. The right lung appears larger than the left lung as it has more lobes. This is to make space for the heart.

8. Hairs in the nose help to clean the air that is breathed in.

9. Bony plates in the nasal cavity of the skull are covered in mucus membrane, which helps to trap dust and bacteria and to warm up the air and moisten it before it reaches the lungs.

10. Through breathing, the equivalent of several cups of water (about 0.5 dm³) a day are lost from the body.

11. The fastest sneeze recorded is 102 miles per hour.

> **Measuring lung volume**
>
> *Ask pupil's to take some measurements of their own lung volumes using a spirometer. Ask them to compare their results. They should find that females and shorter people have a lower lung volume. No spirometer? Exhale through a tube into a large container full of water, inverted over a trough or sink of water.*

the journey so far

During Key Stage 2, pupils should have learnt:

- the common names of some bones
- animals have a skeleton to support their body and protect their organs
- the skull protects the brain, ribs protect the lungs and backbone protects the spinal cord
- an animal's skeleton helps it to move because muscles are attached to bones
- muscles work in pairs: one contracts as one relaxes
- a human skeleton is made of bone and grows as they grow
- the skeleton bends at joints
- animals such as crabs have an exoskeleton.

Some pupils may know about different types of joint, for example that the hip is a ball and socket joint.

the science at key stage 3

The skeletal system consists of bones and the tissues (tendons, ligaments and cartilage) which connect or protect them.

The skeleton

The adult human skeleton consists of 206 bones. The main parts are the skull, backbone, rib cage, limbs and limb girdles. The skeleton has three main roles in the body:

- to support soft tissues
- to protect vital organs
- to act as a set of levers to aid movement.

Bones

Bone is made up of cells embedded in a matrix of calcium and other minerals. As a living tissue, it has its own blood supply, is constantly being dissolved and replaced, and has the ability to repair itself if broken. Exercise and a balanced diet with adequate calcium, phosphate and vitamin D are needed to ensure a healthy skeleton.

Minerals make it a very hard material, but fibres in the structure prevent it from being brittle. It has high tensile strength and can resist blows and bending.

Teeth are also considered part of the skeletal system, but they are made of enamel and dentine, not bone.

Support

Without bones, the body would be 'floppy', like a jellyfish. All the organs would be contained within a skin 'sack' but there would be no definite structure. For example, the backbone (vertebral column) allows a person to stand upright.

Protection

The skeleton protects a number of organs from being damaged. These include:

- skull – protects the brain
- ribcage – protects the heart and lungs
- back bone – protects the spinal cord.

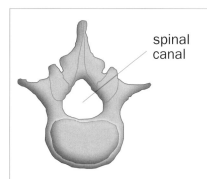

Each vertebra in the backbone has a hole through its centre for the spinal cord, so that it is protected on all sides.

Movement of the skeleton

Muscles attached to bones contract to cause movement.

Joints

Movement between bones occurs at joints, although some bones in the skeleton are fixed, such as in the cranium of the skull, or only slightly movable, such as between the vertebrae.

There are several types of freely movable joint, allowing different kinds of movement. For example:

- hinge joints found at the knee and elbow, allow movement backwards and forwards
- ball and socket joints found at the hip and shoulder, allow rotation.

Bones are attached together by ligaments. These contain elastic fibres and can stretch very slightly. The ends of bones are covered by smooth but very tough cartilage. This reduces friction to prevent the bones from wearing excessively. Rubbing is further prevented by the presence of synovial fluid, which lubricates the joint.

Antagonistic muscles

Muscles are connected to bones by tendons, which contain strong but inelastic collagen fibres. When a muscle contracts it shortens, pulling on a bone. It cannot expand and push, so movement at a joint is controlled by a pair of antagonistic muscles working in opposition. When one contracts to cause movement, the other is relaxed and stretched back to its original shape. For example:

to bend the arm:

- the biceps muscle contracts
- the triceps muscle relaxes and stretches

to straighten the arm:

- the biceps muscle relaxes and stretches
- the triceps muscle contracts.

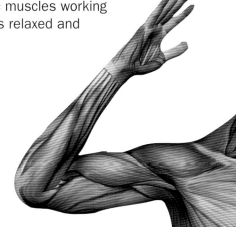

the journey ahead

During Key Stage 4, pupils will learn about the skeletal system in much greater detail. They will study:

- the correct anatomical names of some bones in the body
- the detailed structure of certain bones, such as the vertebral column
- how different joints allow movement, including pivot, saddle and gliding joints
- how bones grow through the process of ossification.

This topic will be explored in even greater detail if a pupil chooses to study GCSE Physical Education.

teaching issues

Vocabulary and use of language

Although it is not essential to use technical language, many pupils are interested and able to do so.

Common use of anatomical terms

Many new anatomical terms can be used in this topic and many pupils will have heard some of these terms used before in everyday situations. At Key Stage 3, pupils only need to use the common names for some bones. However, those familiar with anatomical names should be encouraged to use these terms. This will be particularly likely if a child is enthused by watching or playing sport, or they have broken a bone! A case in point is that knee cap, for which the correct term is the patella.

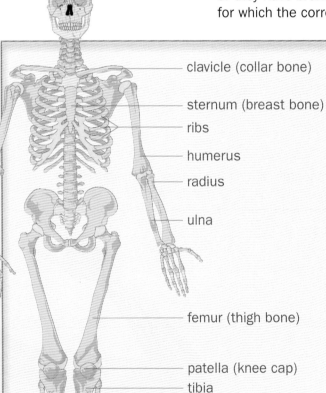

clavicle (collar bone)

sternum (breast bone)

ribs

humerus

radius

ulna

femur (thigh bone)

patella (knee cap)

tibia

fibula

The diagram, left, shows some of the bone names that pupils might learn – it is not an exhaustive list. Note that not all have a common name.

Self-portrait

To encourage a better understanding of the nature of the skeleton and to introduce the names of some of the bones, have pupils sketch a 'self-portrait' of their own skeleton. Ask them to label the bones they know. Then compare it with a full size plastic skeleton or diagram. What did they get right and wrong?

Then – label each other!

Provide pupils with post-it notes, each containing the name of a bone. They then stick these onto a partner in the correct position. To make this more difficult, use the correct anatomical name rather than the common name. An example is scapula, instead of shoulder blade.

Confusion between tendons and ligaments

Pupils find it very difficult to remember the difference between tendons and ligaments:

- tendons join muscle to bone
- ligaments join bone to bone

Get them to make up a rhyme, mnemonic or other fact to remember the difference. One idea might be: tendon contains six letters, so does muscle – tendons must join muscles to bone.

Investigating joints

Some pupils find it difficult to comprehend how muscles cause movements at joints. They find it hard to take on board the need for antagonistic pairs because muscles can only contract.

Working muscles

Ask pupils to work in pairs. One partner moves a joint (for example, bend their knee or elbow). The other pupil feels the muscles moving in their leg or arm as their partner bends and straightens the limb. They should feel the muscle shorten and get fatter as the muscle contracts. They should be able to feel the other muscle in the pair become thinner as it is stretched. Note: pair off pupils sensitively and do not make anyone do this if they don't want to.

triceps (contracted)

biceps (contracted)

biceps (relaxed)

triceps (relaxed)

Modelling joints

Elastic bands make good models of muscles. An elastic band has to be stretched before it can contract.

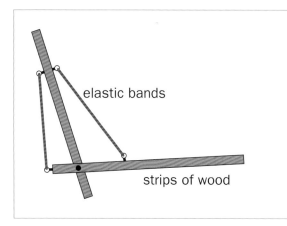

elastic bands

strips of wood

This is a very simple model arm. The elastic bands represent the biceps and triceps muscles. Pupils could be asked to make simple models like this to aid their understanding of movement at a joint.

Joint structure

Some pupils think that the ligaments in joints are just like hinges on a door. They find it hard to imagine the fluid filled joint capsule. Diagrams also make it appear that there is a lot of synovial fluid in a big gap.

1. Use a dissection of a chicken leg to show
   - the external structure of a joint
   - the cartilage over the end of the bones
   - how closely the ends of the bones fit together.
2. Ask them what they think the biggest joint is (the knee). Use water to show how much synovial fluid it contains (0.5 cm^3).

Misconceptions

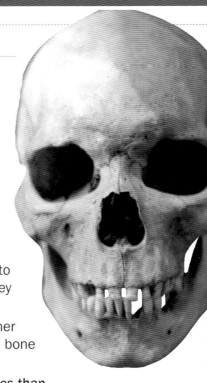

Misconception: Bones are white.
Most pupils believe that bones are pure white, as this is often how they are depicted in illustrations. Bones are not white. They are light yellow or pale brown in colour, as in this photograph of a human skull.

The 'bones are white' misconception is often reinforced when looking at bones in a school collection. Bones are usually bleached as part of the cleaning process, making them safe to handle. When bones are bleached they become white.

The relative quantities of calcium, other minerals and blood cells present in a bone define its colour.

Misconception: Adults have more bones than children. Some pupils think that, as you grow bigger, you have more bones. Actually, you have fewer bones. A baby is born with approximately 300 bones. An adult has 206 bones.

Human brains grow, so a baby's skull has to be flexible. A baby's skull also has to compress to allow it to pass through the birth canal. The bony plates of the cranium fuse together after birth.

The ability of bones to increase rapidly in size is essential for growth. The heads of immature long bones are separated from the shafts by cartilage, which can grow more rapidly than bone.

The differences between growing bones and mature bones can be clearly seen in X-ray images.

In a child, cartilage is constantly replaced by bone (a process known as ossification). Once this process is complete, bones cannot grow longer and the child will have reached their maximum height.

Misconception: The nose has bone inside it.
The common accident of 'breaking your nose' leads pupils to the conclusion that their nose has a bone inside it. In fact, the structure of the nose (and ears) comes from a piece of cartilage, which is far more flexible than bone. If the nose had a bone inside it, many more children and adults would suffer from a broken nose!

Show them a skull and/or X-ray pictures to make the lack of a nose bone clear.

> ### Squashy skulls
>
> *Ask pupils who can to bring pictures of themselves, that show the tops of their heads when newborn and then when older. Some may have been born with very pointed heads, showing how squashy their skulls were!*

Misconception: Bones are made of a dead material. Many pupils believe that bones are made of a dead material. This is encouraged by the fact that the bones pupils have seen and handled are from dead organisms and are often dry, hard, and possibly crumbly. The bones present in a living skeleton, however, are alive, growing and changing all the time like other parts of the body.

Explain that broken bones can mend because they are living. Encourage pupils to recognise bones as organs with a blood supply and made up from a number of living tissues, including bone marrow. Most bones contain a number of layers:

- Periosteum – the outer layer. This thin, dense membrane contains nerves and blood vessels which nourish the bone.

- Compact bone – smooth and very hard. This is the part that is visible when you look at a skeleton.

- Spongy (cancellous) bone – looks a bit like a sponge. Present as layers in the compact bone. It is not as hard as compact bone, but it is still very strong.

- Bone marrow – a thick, jelly-like substance. It makes blood cells.

applications and implications

Scientists at work

Radiographer

There are two types of radiographer – diagnostic and therapeutic. Radiographers require a detailed knowledge of anatomy, physiology and pathology to carry out their work, as well as the skills to use a range of technology.

Diagnostic radiographers look at injuries and disease. They are involved in diagnosing abnormalities such as broken bones, blocked arteries and problems with babies developing in the womb.

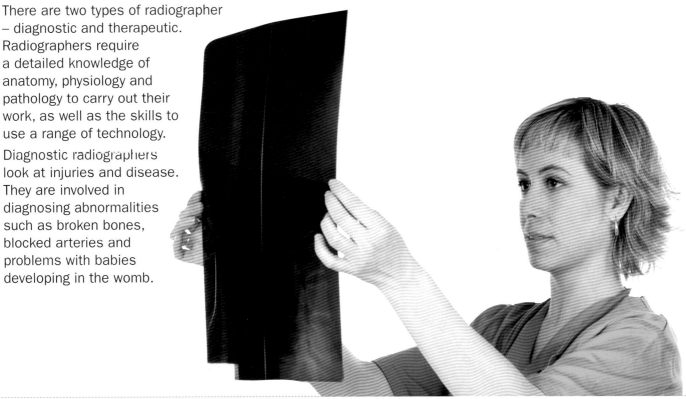

Diagnositc radiographers use many different technologies, including:

X-Ray to look through tissues to examine bones, cavities and foreign objects. Fluoroscopy for images of the digestive system in real-time. Computed Tomography (CT) scanning for cross-sectional views through the body. Magnetic Resonance Imaging (MRI) to build a 2D or 3D map of the different body tissue types. Ultrasound to study fetal development, and to examine organs within the body. Angiography to investigate blood vessels.

Therapeutic radiographers treat patients with cancer by delivering doses of X-rays and other ionising radiation to the tumour. Their aim is to deliver an accurate dose of radiation to the cancer whilst minimising the dose received by the surrounding tissues. Radiographers work with doctors to establish where the area to be treated is located and work out the exact dosage required.

hot topics

Arthritic hands

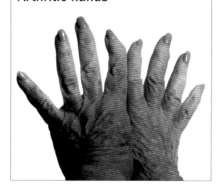

Alternative treatments for arthritis

Arthritis is an illness that causes pain, swelling and loss of movement in joints. It occurs more frequently in older people, though one in a thousand children in the UK are affected. As life expectancy is increasing, more people are becoming afflicted by this condition. There are two hundred kinds of arthritis. The two most common are osteoarthritis and rheumatoid arthritis.

Osteoarthritis normally develops with age and most often affects the fingers, knees, and hips. Sometimes osteoarthritis follows an injury to a joint which occurred in younger life. The cartilage that covers the ends of bones in the joint deteriorates, causing pain and loss of movement as bone begins to rub against bone.

Rheumatoid arthritis happens when the body's own defence system doesn't work properly. The joint lining becomes inflamed as part of the body's immune system activity. It affects joints, bones, and organs – often the hands and feet. It can also cause a person to feel sick or tired, and suffer from a fever.

Increasingly people are looking for natural treatment options (alternative therapies). Many are popular but not all are fully endorsed for effectiveness and safety. Common treatments include:

· acupuncture – to relieve pain and increase movements at joints
· natural supplements – taken to strengthen cartilage and joints, resulting in improved flexibility, bone strength, and pain relief
· osteopathy – massage techniques to reduce pain and swelling
· chiropractics – manipulation of joints, muscles and tendons to provide pain relief.

Prosthetic limbs

The type of prosthesis used depends on the position of the missing limb. Artificial limbs may be needed as a result of a birth defect or from an accident or disease.

The materials used to make prosthetic limbs have improved significantly over the past century. The first artificial limbs were made out of iron, or carved from wood. In recent years, doctors and engineers have worked together to create artificial limbs using composite materials. They move and appear more realistic and are more comfortable to wear.

photo by elvar pálsson licensed under creative commons attribution 2.0

Oscar Pistorius tried to make history by becoming the first double amputee sprinter to compete in the 2008 Olympic Games. Some people did not want Pistorius to be able to compete as they believed his shock-absorbing carbon-fibre prosthetics give him an unfair advantage.

facts and figures

Twelve facts about the skeletal system.

1. At birth a baby has more than 300 bones, but only 206 bones when they are an adult.
2. A broken bone will take around 12 weeks to heal.
3. Every second, the bodies' bone marrow produces approximately two million red blood cells.
4. The smallest bone in the human body is the stirrup bone in the middle ear. It is approximately 0.28 cm long.
5. The femur is the longest and strongest bone in the human body. It is around 50 cm long, and can support up to 30 times the weight of the adult.
6. The masseter muscles in the jaw are the strongest muscles in the human body for their size.
7. There are around 650 muscles in the human body.
8. There are five types of bones in the human body – long, short, flat, irregular and sesamoid.
9. Half of a person's bones are found in their hands and feet.
10. When a body decays, the soft tissues, including the joints and cartilage, rot away. Skeletons fall apart and do not remain intact as shown in films such as *Indiana Jones*.
11. The body contains more calcium than any other mineral.

| 7 | adolescence and reproduction

the journey so far

During Key Stage 2, pupils should have learnt:

- that animals reproduce and change as they get older
- the main stages in the life cycle of a human being
- that children develop into an adult during adolescence (puberty)
- that adults can reproduce by making babies.

The extent of their knowledge will vary according to the sex education policies of their schools and contribution of their parents/carers.

the science at key stage 3

During adolescence, a child develops into an adult. Many physical and psychological changes take place (puberty refers to the biological changes). At the end of adolescence the reproductive system is fully mature and ready to reproduce.

The male reproductive system

The functions of the male reproductive system are to produce sperm and insert them into the female reproductive tract to enable the fertilisation of an egg cell. Main parts of the male reproductive system:

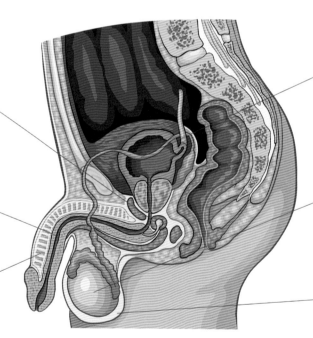

glands – produce fluid containing nutrients which enable the sperm to swim and survive

urethra – tube which carries semen or urine out of the body

penis – organ which passes semen into a woman's vagina during sexual intercourse or urine out of the body

sperm ducts – tubes which carry the sperm from the testes to the urethra; when the sperm mixes with the fluid produced in the glands, it is known as semen

testes (singular testis) – produce sperm and the male hormone testosterone

scrotum – bag of skin which contains the testes

The hazards of tight trousers

The rather vulnerable position of the testes in the scrotum outside the body, compared with the well-protected ovaries, is due to the need for rapid cell division to make sperm at a prodigious rate. This needs a temperature about 2 °C lower than body core temperature. Tight trousers may raise the temperature and can cause infertility.

The female reproductive system

Main parts of the female reproductive system:

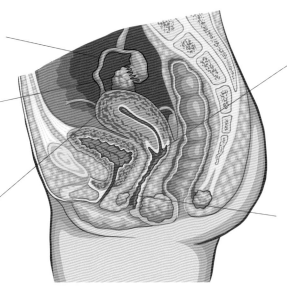

oviduct (egg tubes) – tube which the egg cell travels through on its journey to the uterus

ovaries – contain immature egg cells (ova) and produce the female hormones oestrogen and progesterone

uterus (womb) – muscular bag where a baby develops during pregnancy

cervix – ring of muscle at the bottom of the uterus. This keeps the baby in the uterus during pregnancy until it is ready to be born

vagina – muscular tube that leads from the vagina to the outside of the body. The penis is inserted into the vagina during sexual intercourse

Adolescence

Adolescence in males is triggered by the hormone testosterone and in females by oestrogen. The child's body, designed for growth, is replaced by the adult body, designed for reproduction. Male and female reproductive systems become fully mature and other physical changes occur, with most adolescents undergoing emotional changes and a growth spurt.

Adolescence normally takes place between the ages of eight and fifteen with much individual variation. During adolescence, males and females will grow more hair on their body, under their arms and in the pubic region. Body sweat will also have a stronger smell. A deodorant can prevent unwanted body odour. There are also a number of changes which occur only in males or only in females. The distinguishing changes that don't occur in the reproductive organs themselves are known as secondary sexual characteristics.

physical changes which only take place in males	physical changes which only take place in females
voice becomes noticably deeper when it 'breaks'	breasts develop
testes and penis get bigger	ovaries start to release eggs
testes start to produce sperm	uterus enlarges and menstruation begins
shoulders get wider	hips get wider
hair grows on the face and chest	

the journey ahead

During Key Stage 4, pupils learn about the reproductive system in much greater detail. They study:

- a more detailed structure of the male and female reproductive system
- how the hormones oestrogen, progesterone, LH and FSH control the menstrual cycle
- how genetic information is passed on from parents to their offspring (this is first introduced in this book in *chapter 11: variation and classification*)
- the differences between asexual and sexual reproduction.

teaching issues

Vocabulary and use of language

Common use of anatomical terms

There are lots of new terms used in this topic. Many pupils will have heard them before, as they are regularly referred to in everyday situations. For example, girls have periods. In most cases these more common terms (such as womb) are sufficient for pupils to use at Key Stage 3. However, the more able should be challenged to use the correct anatomical terms (such as uterus). The use of slang terms and colloquialisms should not be allowed.

Reproductive diagrams

Give pupils plenty of opportunities to label structures in both male and female reproductive systems to learn the correct words and understand the structures. Pupils should see diagrams from both a front and side angle. Try asking pupils what they think common terms may mean, before giving them the answer. This may also help to draw out any misconceptions.

> **Reproductive terms**
>
> *Hide reproductive terms such as uterus and testis in a word search. Or, try providing pupils with the answers to a crossword. Pupils then write the clues. The more opportunities pupils get to use the words, the easier they will remember them.*

Dealing with sensitive issues

Before teaching this topic you should ensure you are familiar with your school's sex education policy. You should approach the topic from a scientific perspective, but will need to be aware of the need for sensitivity to the personal circumstances of pupils and their families.

> **Question box**
>
> *A question box can be a good way of pupils asking questions they may find embarrassing to ask in front of their peers. It also allows the teacher to select which questions they may or may not wish to answer.*

Misconceptions

Misconception: Girls produce oestrogen, boys produce testosterone. Oestrogen is often called the female hormone and testosterone, the male hormone. Actually, females and males produce both oestrogen and testosterone. The difference is in the amounts of each hormone they produce. Females produce more oestrogen and males produce more testosterone.

Misconception: A male's voice breaks during adolescence. During adolescence, both male and female voices deepen – they do not actually 'break'. It is much more noticeable in males as their voices may deepen by up to an octave, whereas a female voice usually only deepens by a couple of tones. As the voice deepens, some males initially find it difficult to control the pitch of their voice, giving the idea that their voice is breaking.

The larynx (voice box) is made of cartilage. Stretched across it are two muscles known as vocal cords. As air is forced out of the lungs it passes between the vocal cords, making them vibrate to produce sounds.

During adolescence testosterone causes the cartilage to grow larger and thicker. At the same time, the vocal cords also grow longer and thicker. They now vibrate at a lower frequency producing a deeper sound. As these changes occur, the larynx tilts to a different angle in the neck and protrudes forwards. This forms a prominent 'Adam's apple'.

Misconception: Males can pass urine during sexual intercourse. In males, the urethra can pass both urine and semen out of the body. However, this does not occur at the same time. An involuntary ring of muscle present at the base of the bladder (called the internal urethral sphincter) automatically closes when orgasmic contractions begin. This prevents urine leaving and semen entering the bladder. Urination during erection is possible prior to this but, normally, voluntary control of the muscles that compress the urethra at the base of the bladder prevents this happening.

Misconception: All teenagers undergo adolescence at approximately the same time. Adolescence is a transient stage which takes place between childhood and adulthood. It involves both physical and psychological changes. Physical changes are much easier to measure than psychological ones, but it is still very difficult to determine when adolescence begins and ends. Generally these changes take place between the ages of eight and fifteen. The average age for onset is eleven for girls and twelve for boys. However, there can be great variation – for example, girls usually start menstruating two to three years after the onset of puberty and at any time between around eight and sixteen years old. Girls also develop more rapidly, reaching full maturity in about four years, while boys take about six years.

Misconception: Having sexual intercourse during pregnancy will damage the developing baby. If a woman is having a normal pregnancy then it is considered safe for her to have sexual intercourse at all stages of pregnancy. The developing baby cannot be damaged as it will not come into contact with the penis during sexual intercourse. The baby is protected by the amniotic sac (the bag that contains the fetus and amniotic fluid) and the strong muscles of the uterus. There is also a thick mucus plug which seals the cervix. This ensures the baby remains in the correct position and helps protect the baby from infection.

The presence of an Adam's apple shows that a male voice has 'broken' – this normally takes place between the ages of eleven and fifteen.

applications and implications

Science at home – dealing with adolescence

Spots and acne treatment

During adolescence, testosterone stimulates sebaceous glands in the skin to produce excessive sebum. Sebum appears to be important in maintaining the coat of hairy mammals, but the function of sebum in humans is a matter of debate. Young children have no sebaceous glands, but healthy skin. It has been suggested that sebum helps to waterproof the skin and provides a medium for the growth of 'friendly' bacteria – but some think its sole function is to cause acne! The glands easily become blocked by dead skin cells. As sebum is still being produced, this causes a swelling. Bacteria may invade the area and release toxins, causing pus-filled spots to erupt. Spots normally occur on the face, neck, chest and back. Acne is a more severe problem. This occurs when crops of pustules erupt on the face and other body areas.

Many believe chocolate, junk food and fried food cause spots, but scientists have never proven this link. Stress and tiredness tend to increase the appearance of spots. Teenagers should be encouraged not to squeeze spots as this tends to make the spots more inflamed and can spread infection and cause scarring. To reduce the outbreak of spots, adolescents should be encouraged to cleanse their face thoroughly with water-based cleansing lotions. Alcohol-based lotions can cause dry skin, irritation and peeling. A well balanced diet and exposure to sunshine can help reduce spots. More severe cases of acne can be treated with prescribed medicines, such as antibiotics and hormone treatments.

Preventing body odour

Sweating is important – it helps prevent the body from overheating. There are two kinds of sweat gland, most of which produce sweat which is mainly salt and water. Sweat itself is odourless. Body odour is caused when bacteria living on the skin break down sweat and dead skin cells. This process releases chemicals which cause an unpleasant smell. Young children do not normally have body odour but, in puberty, new sweat glands develop in the armpits and genital area. These cause more body odour, because they produce proteins and oily substances that bacteria feed on and break down. Feet enclosed in socks and shoes produce their own smell because fungi, as well as bacteria, flourish in the humid environment. If clothes get sweaty, bacteria can make them smelly too.

To prevent body odour, a person must wash themselves and their clothes regularly. However, skin is normally slightly acid (pH 4.5-6) to inhibit bacterial growth. Alkaline soaps raise the pH and encourage bacteria to grow, so rinsing soap away is important.

Acne leaflet

Ask pupils to produce a leaflet for other adolescents, dispelling the myths about spots. It should contain useful information on why teenagers get spots and how to prevent them.

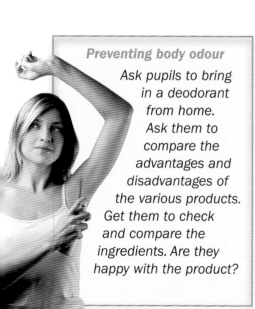

Preventing body odour

Ask pupils to bring in a deodorant from home. Ask them to compare the advantages and disadvantages of the various products. Get them to check and compare the ingredients. Are they happy with the product?

Deodorants are used by many people to reduce body odour. Some simply mask the smell, though others contain anti-bacterial agents. Antiperspirants can be used to help reduce sweating, and some also inhibit bacterial growth. Most antiperspirants are aluminium based. They contain, for example, aluminium chloride, aluminium chlorohydrate or aluminium-zirconium compounds. These react with the salts in sweat to form a gel plug that blocks sweat glands and reduces sweating.

Coping with periods

Some women find periods painful. This is normally caused by prostaglandins. These cause the muscle of the uterus to 'cramp' which helps shed the lining of the uterus. Discomfort can be eased by taking painkillers, applying a hot water bottle to the area or exercising. Exercise helps by releasing endorphins – chemicals in the body which make you feel better.

There are two main types of sanitary protection:

Tampons – a small compacted absorbent cloth. This is inserted into the vagina. It must be changed at least every eight hours and can be worn during swimming. There is a very slightly increased risk of toxic shock syndrome (a disease caused by bacteria) whilst using this product. However, the disease is extremely rare and risk is minimal if tampons are changed regularly.

Sanitary towels – a piece of absorbent cloth worn outside the body. They are hygienic and do not leak if changed regularly.

Scientists at work

School nurse

The school nurse's role focuses on four main areas:

Exercise and healthy eating – this aims to combat obesity problems and to prevent, identify and treat eating disorders.

Mental health and wellbeing – this includes helping pupils with depression and bullying issues. Some pupil's undergoing adolescence before or after the majority of their peers may be a target for bullying.

Sexual health and relationships – this includes dealing with teenage pregnancy, and providing advice on contraception and sexually transmitted diseases.

Recreational drug abuse – this includes offering advice and mechanisms for stopping pupils taking drugs, drinking alcohol and smoking.

Urban myth

The rumour that antiperspirants caused breast cancer was widely spread through the internet. There is no scientific evidence from the research that has been done, though this belief still persists. Have pupils do an internet search to find some of the very convincing websites. Use this to discuss how you can recognise or check for reputable sources.

The school nurse

Most schools have their own school nurse, or one who attends the school regularly. Schools should provide a drop-in or booking service to meet with the nurse to discuss adolescence issues. Counselling and advice will be given in confidence. The pupil would be referred to external bodies such as their GP if necessary. Pupils should be encouraged to make use of this service if they have any concerns, however small the problem.

history and culture

After a child has passed through adolescence they are deemed to be an adult. By this time, as well as undergoing large physical changes, they should have developed mentally and emotionally to be able to cope with making 'adult decisions'.

Religious ceremonies

In some cultures (particularly in the past), ceremonies are performed to celebrate an individual becoming an adult. Examples include:

Seijin shiki – an adult ceremony which takes place in Japan.

Upanayanam – a coming of age ceremony for Hindu males.

Bat or Bar Mitzvah – coming of age ceremonies for Jews. These take place for twelve-year-old girls (Bat Mitzvah) and thirteen-year-old boys (Bar Mitzvah).

Confirmation – a ceremony in which individuals (normally adolescents) confirm their beliefs and become members of the Christian church in their own right.

Many tribes include ceremonies where promises are made by adolescents to avoid shaming their family or village as the child enters adulthood.

Nowadays, many people believe events such as passing your driving test, leaving school or gaining your first full time job are more important factors in showing that a person has become an adult.

> **Cross-curricular opportunity**
>
> *Cross-curricular links can be made with religious studies, charting how different cultures mark the progression from childhood to adulthood.*

Youth culture

Through articles in the popular press, many adults gain a perception of youth which is often biased or incorrect. Stories of youth crime, the rise in numbers of youths carrying knives and guns and anti-social behaviour contribute to this perception.

What is not news-worthy is the important role that adolescents played in movements which have resulted in positive social change throughout history, back to Joan of Arc and beyond. In modern times, a rising voice of youth activism is being heard, effecting political, moral, social and educational change. Youth-led organisations are pressing for change at an ever-increasing pace, backed by the United Nations Convention on the Rights of the Child. Young adults often take gap years, undertaking voluntary work to help others, often in other societies.

The United Nations Convention on the Rights of the Child is an international convention setting out the civil, political, economic, social and cultural rights of children. Almost every country in the world, with the notable exception of the USA, has signed up to the convention. This legally binding document secures youth participation throughout society, while imposing controls on the use of child labour. It came into force on 02 September 1990.

Legal ages

Criminal responsibility: In England, the legal age of criminal responsibility is ten. A child above this age is legally regarded as an adult, and can be held responsible for their actions. Below this age they are considered too young to be held accountable for criminal action. This defence is called *doli incapax* – incapable of crime. This age varies from seven (in India and South Africa) to eighteen (in Belgium).

Working age: In the UK, people between fourteen and sixteen can carry out work which fits in around school hours, for up to twelve hours per week. After sixteen, this can become full-time employment, though there are plans to raise the school leaving age to eighteen in 2013.

Consent to sexual activity: The age of consent to sexual activity in the UK is sixteen for both heterosexual and homosexual relationships. As recently as 2000, the age of consent for homosexual activity was higher (previously at eighteen years of age). Sexual intercourse with a person below the age of consent is a criminal act punishable with a prison sentence.

Marriage: In England, as in the majority of the world, people can get married from the age of eighteen, or sixteen with parental consent (not needed in Scotland). In Japan, parental consent is needed until twenty years of age.

Eligibility to vote: The age of universal suffrage (when all citizens are entitled to vote) is eighteen for most countries. It is sixteen in Guernsey, Jersey and the Isle of Man.

Purchasing cigarettes and alcohol: In the UK, sales of these products are limited to eighteen years old and above. In reality, it is common that adolescents engage in smoking or drinking below these ages. In many cultures this is tolerated to a certain degree. However, public pressure due to the rises in binge drinking and public order offences may lead to a revision in the law.

Driving: In the UK, the minimum driving age is seventeen. While learning to drive a person must drive a car displaying L plates. Australia has a graduated system of learning plates. A driver must display L plates from age sixteen, and drive only under supervision from a licensed driver, red P plates demonstrating they possess a probationary license at seventeen and green P plates at eighteen.

Debate activity

Is a seventeen-year old physically and psychologically mature enough to drive a car? This question could be the stimulus for a class debate on the differing rates of maturity among young adults of different ages, among the sexes and among individuals. Try playing 'devil's advocate' to challenge pupil's preconceptions of physical and psychological maturity.

Linking with PSHE

As a child becomes an adult, so their responsibilities to society increase. The links between physical, emotional and psychological maturity and a person's position in society can be established. This can form a particularly effective study in partnership with a school's PSHE programme.

Debate activity

The UK has the highest teenage birth rates in Western Europe – six times higher than in the Netherlands. Hold a debate as to whether increasing the age of consent to eighteen would help to reduce the amount of teenage pregnancies. Do pupils have any other suggestions for tackling this issue?

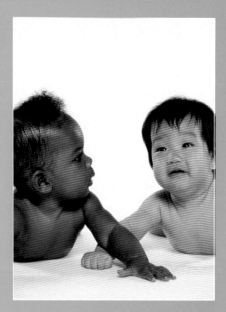

the journey so far

During Key Stage 2, pupils should have learnt:

- that animals reproduce and change as they get older
- the main stages in the life cycle of a human being
- that adults reproduce by making babies
- that humans give birth to live young
- the importance of reproduction to prevent species from dying out.

They will know that animals such as birds, frogs or butterflies produce young which grow into adults. They will know that plants produce pollen in a male organ which fertilises an ovum in a female organ. They are likely to know that new life starts in humans and other animals with fertilisation. The extent of their knowledge will vary according to the sex education policies of their schools and the contribution of their parents/carers.

the science at key stage 3

To produce a baby, a sperm must fertilise an egg cell (ovum). For fertilisation to occur, an egg cell must be present in the oviduct. This only occurs for a short period during the menstrual cycle.

The menstrual cycle

An average menstrual cycle lasts 28 days, but for many women, their cycle is slightly longer or shorter than this.

Stages of the menstrual cycle

There are four main stages:

1. The cycle begins (on day one) when bleeding from the vagina occurs. The uterus is shed with a small amount of blood. This is known as menstruation (a period).

2. Menstruation lasts for about five days. The lining of the uterus then begins to re-grow. At the same time, an egg cell starts to mature in one of the ovaries.

3. The egg cell is released from the ovary – ovulation. This occurs half way through the cycle, on approximately day fourteen.

4. The egg cell is carried down the oviduct towards the uterus. The lining of the uterus is now thick and spongy, ready for an embryo to implant. If fertilisation does not occur, the egg cell will disintegrate and the cycle will start again with menstruation.

Cessation of menstruation

If fertilisation takes place in the oviduct, the embryo which forms is carried into the uterus, where it implants itself into the lining (endometrium). The woman is now pregnant.

Menstruation and the continuation of the normal cycle are prevented by the release of the hormone hCG (or HCG, human chorionic gonadotrophin) from embryo cells.

It is the detection of this hormone in urine that forms the basis of pregnancy tests.

Fertilisation

Sperm cell

The sperm cell is much smaller than the egg cell, and has a strong tail for swimming. Most of the head is nucleus, which contains the genetic information from the father. The head also contains enzymes (in the acrosome) to digest the outer surfaces of the egg cell.

During sexual intercourse, millions of sperm are released in semen into the top of the vagina. They swim through the opening in the cervix into the womb (uterus) and then into the oviducts (Fallopian tubes). Only the healthiest sperm get this far.

Egg cell (ovum)

A mature egg cell is much larger than a sperm cell. Its nucleus contains genetic information from the mother. The cytoplasm contains a food store to enable the embryo to start to develop. Each month an egg cell is released from the ovary into the oviduct, where it begins its journey to the uterus.

Fertilisation occurs when the nucleus of the sperm cell and the nucleus of the egg cell join together. The chromosome number returns to its normal 46 (23 pairs). The cell divides to form a ball of cells, the developing embryo.

Pregnancy

The embryo is moved into the uterus, where it implants itself into the lining (endometrium) by secreting enzymes to digest its way in. The woman is now pregnant. During the next nine months, the fertilised egg develops into a baby. About 9 weeks from fertilisation, the organs have formed and the embryo becomes the fetus. The remaining phases up to birth are mainly growth.

The developing baby needs protection, nutrients and oxygen. This is made possible by:

1. Amniotic fluid – This fluid in the amniotic sac in the uterus acts as a shock absorber to prevent the baby from being damaged.
2. Placenta – This allows substances such as oxygen, nutrients and carbon dioxide to pass between the mother's and baby's blood (which never mix).
3. Umbilical cord – Joins the placenta to the baby.

Birth

The baby is ready to be born after about nine months. Hormones stimulate the uterus (a very strong muscle) to contract and the cervix to dilate. The baby is forced out of the mother's body through the very elastic vagina.

the journey ahead

During Key Stage 4, pupils learn about the reproductive system in much greater detail. They study:

- more details of the structure and functions of the male and female reproductive systems
- how the hormones LH, FSH, oestrogen and progesterone control the menstrual cycle
- the acrosomal reaction which occurs when sperm cells meet an egg cell
- how a fetus develops
- how hormones such as oxytocin cause birth.

They will consider advantages of internal fertilisation over external fertilisation and look at details of puberty. They may discuss the ethical issues concerning IVF and the separation of conjoined twins.

teaching issues

> **Development of a fetus**
>
> *Give pupils diagrams or photographs of embryonic and fetal development at different stages of pregnancy. Ask them to sequence the diagrams and label the major structures such as the placenta and umbilical cord.*

Vocabulary and use of language

Conception and implantation

Conception is a term which is often used in the media and by pro-life pressure groups. It is usually used to mean fertilisation, the fusing of the male and female gametes (syngamy). It is significant, because it represents the point at which a new life has been formed, different to the parents. Since the embryo cannot develop until it has implanted, sometimes this is considered to be the point of conception. Much controversy is associated with the debate over when the new life has become truly human and if and when abortion is morally acceptable.

Common use of anatomical terms

The new terms associated with this topic may already have been encountered by many pupils. You could try asking them what they think common terms may mean; this can also help to draw out any misconceptions. In most cases, common terms (such as womb) are sufficient for pupils to use at this level. However, the use of slang terms and colloquialisms should not be allowed.

Challenge the more able to use the correct anatomical terms (such as uterus).

Note: Although 'foetus' is still in common use, the correct spelling is now held to be 'fetus'.

Dealing with sensitive issues

Before teaching this topic, teachers should ensure they are familiar with their school's sex education policy. Teachers should approach the topic from a scientific perspective, but will need to be aware of the need for sensitivity to the personal circumstances of pupils and their families.

Contraception

> **Contraception circus**
>
> *Organise a contraception circus. At each station, pupils should look at a method of contraception, with associated documentation. They should find out how it works, its advantages and disadvantages.*

Pupils should be made aware of different methods of contraception. For each method they should be able to explain in simple terms how it prevents pregnancy. This topic will also be discussed in personal, social and health education (PSHE) lessons. Some religions forbid the use of certain methods of contraception. This can be brought to the pupils' attention for discussion.

Misconceptions (no pun intended)

Misconception: Pregnancy lasts nine months. Many pupils believe pregnancy lasts nine months. This is actually a generalisation. Pregnancy is measured from the date of the start of the woman's last period. The time of fertilisation is very hard to pinpoint, as most women are unaware of the time they ovulate. A standard pregnancy is defined as lasting 40 weeks. About 90% of women give birth between 38-42 weeks.

Misconception: Lots of blood is lost during a woman's period. A period occurs as a result of the body shedding the endometrium lining of the uterus. A small amount of blood is lost but most of the discharge is the uterine lining. On average, a woman loses 35 cm^3 of blood. 10-80 cm^3 of blood loss in a period is considered normal. Nonetheless, this is enough to deplete iron reserves, so a good diet is needed to replace the loss and prevent anaemia.

Misconception: A baby grows in a woman's tummy. Many people use 'tummy' to describe where a baby is developing as an alternative word for the abdomen. As tummy is also a term used to refer to the stomach, the use of this description is very misleading. A baby does develop within a woman's abdomen but, more specifically, inside the uterus.

Misconception: The circulation of the mother and the fetus are connected. The circulatory systems are separate, with the placenta acting as a barrier as well as being designed to allow important substances such as food and waste to pass through. A functioning heart is therefore one of the first organs to develop.

Misconception: Sperm have a brain. Some pupils believe sperm have a brain which enables them to know where to swim to find the egg. Sperm do contain a nucleus, but this is not a brain. It contains genetic information which will be passed on from a father to its offspring. The precise method by which a sperm locates the egg cell is still being researched. The sperm respond to chemicals in their environment. Current research suggests that sperm can 'smell' the egg.

Misconception: It takes millions of sperm to fertilise an egg. It only takes one sperm to fertilise an egg. Millions of sperm are released with each ejaculation, to increase the chances of a woman becoming pregnant. They are produced so fast that many are incompletely formed or immature. Lots of sperm have damaged flagella (tails) and can't swim far enough. Some are too old, as they could have been stored in the testes for several days before ejaculation. Therefore, only the strongest and healthiest sperm cells will reach the egg. It is then a race to burrow into the egg cell first. Once the head of one sperm enters the egg cell, a chemical reaction occurs preventing any others from entering the egg cell.

Doctors use pregnancy calculators to calculate due dates. They turn the arrow to the date of the woman's last period. The other arrow will then point to the date her baby is due.

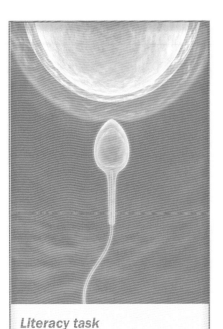

Literacy task

Ask pupils to imagine they are a sperm cell. They need to describe the journey they would take from their production in the testis to fertilising an egg.

applications and implications

A home pregnancy test

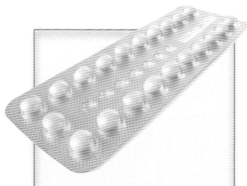

Research opportunity

Pupils could research the long term health benefits and risks of taking the contraceptive pill. Ask them to compare the advantages and disadvantages of taking the mini-pill over the combined pill.

Science at home

Pregnancy tests

Many women first discover that they are pregnant by carrying out a home pregnancy test. Home pregnancy tests are designed to detect human chorionic gonadotropin (hCG) in urine. This is a hormone released by the embryo after it implants into the uterine lining, and then by the placenta when it has formed. The hormone is excreted by the kidneys. Its presence in urine normally causes a line or word to appear on a pregnancy tester.

The contraceptive pill

Many women take the oral contraceptive pill on a daily basis to prevent unwanted pregnancies. Before taking the pill, a doctor must carry out important health checks to determine their suitability. There are two types of contraceptive pill:

Combined pill – contains both oestrogen and progesterone. It works by inhibiting ovulation and thickening the mucus around the cervix. This makes it difficult for sperm to enter the uterus and reach any eggs that may have been released. The hormones can also affect the lining of the uterus, making it difficult for a fertilised egg to implant into the wall of the uterus.

Mini-pill – contains only progesterone. It works by altering the cervical mucus and the lining of the uterus.

Scientists at work

Midwives

Midwives provide support and care for a woman and her family during pregnancy and up to the first month after birth. They need to have a full understanding of the female reproductive system and the changes which take place during pregnancy.

At each appointment, a midwife will perform a number of checks to ensure that a pregnancy is proceeding normally. If they spot any abnormalities, a woman will be referred to an obstetrician. The two professions should complement each other. However, often there are fundamental disagreements because obstetricians are taught to 'actively manage' labour, whereas midwives try to allow labour to occur naturally and only intervene if necessary.

Sonographers

Sonographers use ultrasonic imaging devices to produce diagnostic images and scans. To perform this skill effectively, sonographers must have a good understanding of ultrasound physics, anatomy, physiology and pathology.

One of the most common uses of ultrasound is to check the development of the fetus during pregnancy. The diameter of the cranium gives a good indication of the stage of pregnancy. Sonographers check the position of the placenta to ensure that it is not blocking the cervix – if so, a baby will need to be delivered by caesarean section as it will not be able to pass through the cervix and into the vagina. Ultrasound technology can also be used to check how many babies are present, to measure the size and estimate the weight of baby, and to check for various abnormalities.

Fertility specialists

Fertility specialists provide help to couples who are having trouble conceiving naturally. There are a range of treatments available depending on the reason for the inability of a couple to conceive. Doctors have to have a detailed knowledge of both the female and the male reproductive system and the stages involved in pregnancy in order to perform their job.

In vitro fertilisation (IVF) is a major treatment used to help infertile couples. A woman is normally given a number of hormone injections to cause many egg cells to reach maturity in one menstrual cycle (normally only one egg cell would reach maturity per month). Using a fine needle, these egg cells are removed from the woman's ovaries. They are then fertilised with sperm in a fluid medium, in the laboratory. The fertilised eggs are left for a few days, to begin development. The embryos which have developed effectively are chosen and transferred to the patient's uterus. Pregnancy, it is hoped, then proceeds naturally. IVF is a very expensive treatment, and cannot guarantee success – success rates are currently around 25% per treatment.

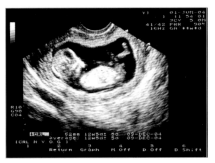

An ultrasound of a baby at approximately 20 weeks. This scan is used to examine a baby's anatomy, to ensure it is developing normally. Particular attention is paid to the brain, face, spine, heart, stomach, bowel, kidneys and limbs. Sometimes people ask to find out the sex of their unborn child, but this is not always possible to see as it depends on the baby's position.

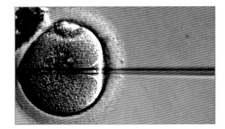

A fine needle is often used to insert a sperm into an egg cell during IVF treatment.

hot topics

Three and four dimensional ultrasound scans

Many women now pay to have three- and four-dimensional ultrasound scans of their unborn child. These techniques provide them with a much clearer picture of what their baby looks like.

Most ultrasounds, routinely performed on women, are two dimensional. They reflect sound waves in a single plane. The ultrasound is directed straight down and reflected back up again. It results in a black and white two dimensional image of the baby.

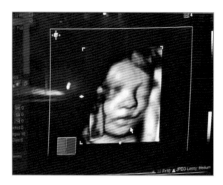

3D ultrasound image of a baby developing in the womb

The baby's facial features can be seen; it has its eyes closed.

3D ultrasounds use a technique called surface rendering. Sound waves are sent down at different angles and their reflections interpreted by sophisticated software. The software produces an instant image of the baby which appears three dimensional, and enables surface details to be seen with remarkable clarity. 4D ultrasound refers to a moving image of the baby. It is produced in the same way as a 3D ultrasound, with rapid updates of the image in real time.

Termination of pregnancies

When abortion was first legalised, abortions were allowed up to twenty eight weeks. In 1990, MPs voted to cut the limit to twenty four weeks. There is still debate over the current time limit.

Three- and four-dimensional ultrasound scanning has re-highlighted this issue, as these techniques have enabled people to see clearly what a baby is able to do at each stage of development. There have also been huge advances in medical care and facilities enabling babies born before twenty four weeks to survive.

In 2007, Amillia Taylor became the youngest premature baby to survive. She was born at twenty one weeks and six days. She weighed just 10 ounces and measured about 24 cm in length.

Pupils could explore their feelings towards terminations through case studies such as Amillia Taylor.

Male contraceptive pill

In the last few years, a vast amount of research has been carried out into the development of a male contraceptive pill. This may take the form of a single pill or a longer-acting implant. The male pill may become widely available in the next few years.

The male contraceptive pill aims to work by blocking sperm production. To achieve this, a combination of the sex hormones progesterone and testosterone will probably be used. This is because high levels of testosterone in a male will prevent sperm production. Research shows that this could also cause unwanted side effects such as acne, weight gain and prostate-gland growth. Too much progesterone in a male will also suppress sperm production but could alter male sexuality and sexual characteristics. A fine balance of testosterone and progesterone, therefore, will have to be found. As it only takes a single sperm to create a new life, scientists are still trying to develop a pill that is 100% effective in blocking sperm production.

Debate activities

Pupils could hold a discussion about the advantages and disadvantages of a male contraceptive pill. Ask males: 'would you be happy to take the male contraceptive pill?' Ask females: 'would you be happy to rely on a male taking the contraceptive pill or would you prefer to be in control of your own fertility?'

Alternatively, pupils could debate on the pros and cons of contraception in general.

1. A fertile male makes about 100 new sperm every second.
2. A sperm swims towards the egg at about three millimetres per minute.
3. The name sperm is derived from the Greek word *sperma*, meaning seed. It is a shortened form of spermatozoon (plural spermatozoa), the name given to a motile male gamete.
4. The average sperm has a head about 3 µm (micrometres) in diameter and a tail about 6 µm long.
5. The fruit fly has the largest known spermatozoon relative to its size. *Drosophila melanogaster* produces sperm that can be up to 1.8 mm in size, which is longer than the adult fly.
6. At about 120-150 µm in diameter, the largest cell in the female human body is the ovum or egg cell.
7. Identical twins are produced when a fertilised egg splits during a very early developmental stage. Identical twins must be of the same sex. Their genetic make up is identical.
8. Non-identical twins are produced when two different sperms fertilise two separate eggs. The twins can be of the same sex or different. They will appear as similar as two siblings.
9. Pregnancy tests used to be carried out by injecting female African clawed toads (*Xenopus*) with urine. If the woman was pregnant, the hormone in their urine caused the toads to lay eggs.

history and culture

Confusion can arise from different spellings of words on different sides of the Atlantic. For example, American textbooks use estrogen rather than oestrogen. Occasionally, entirely different terms are used, for example epinephrine rather than adrenaline.

Foetus or fetus?

The Cambridge doctors Boyd and Hamilton confronted the issue of fetus versus foetus in the 1960s when they wrote a textbook on human embryology with the American Professor Mossman. In a letter to the British Medical Journal, they put the case for fetus. They explained that a Cambridge expert on classical terms, Professor Cook, claimed that fetus was more correct. He dated the error back to Isidorus of Seville (AD 570-636), who assumed the wrong derivation of the word and foetus was copied from him for many centuries. The correct derivation is from feo (I beget), with fetus being first used for fruits by Roman writers such as Virgil and Ovid. The assumption had been that foetus derived from a Greek word rather than from Latin, and the spelling had been maintained more through snobbery than anything else! Nowadays, it is recognised that fetus is not a foible of the Americans and, although the BBC uses both versions indiscriminately, modern medical texts and The Institute of Biology insist on fetus.

| 9 | micro-organisms

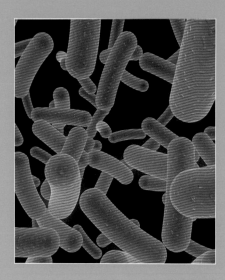

the journey so far

During Key Stage 2, pupils should have learnt:

- micro-organisms are tiny and are only visible with the aid of a microscope
- bacteria and viruses are types of micro-organisms
- some micro-organisms are harmful and cause disease
- some micro-organisms are useful and can be used to make products such as bread and yoghurt, or act as decomposers
- some ways to prevent the spread of micro-organisms.

Although they are likely to know that yeast is used to make bread, they are unlikely to know it is a fungus and that fungi can be micro-organisms.

the science at key stage 3

Micro-organisms (or microbes) can only be seen with the aid of a microscope. They are found wherever life can survive. Most micro-organisms are beneficial. Some can be used to produce useful products for humans and many are important decomposers, essential in recycling materials for the maintenance of ecosystems. Others are harmful and can cause disease; these are called pathogens.

Types of micro-organism

There are three main types of micro-organism:

1. fungi (singular – fungus)
2. bacteria (singular – bacterium)
3. viruses (singular – virus)

At this stage, pupils do not need to know about microscopic plants and animals (Kingdom: Protoctista, which includes single celled or simple multicellular animals and plants such as protozoa and algae).

Fungi

Fungi include yeasts, which are among the largest types of micro-organism. They are single celled organisms, some of which can be used to make beer and bread. Each cell has a nucleus. Fungi also include larger non-microscopic varieties such as mushrooms and toadstools, which make bodies out of branching threads (hyphae).

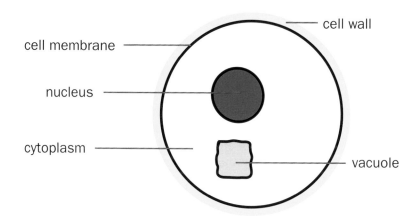

Generalised diagram of a microscopic fungus

Bacteria

Bacteria are generally smaller than fungi. They have a wide range of shapes and may have projections, such as tails (flagella, singular flagellum) to help them swim, and tiny hairs (pili, singular pilus) to help them to attach to surfaces. Instead of a nucleus and chromosomes, they have a circular ring of DNA (nucleoid). Useful bacteria include those used to make cheese and yoghurt.

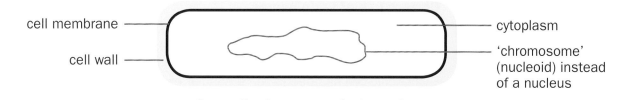

Generalised structure of a bacterium

Viruses

Viruses are the smallest type of micro-organism and are not visible using a light microscope. They do not have a nucleus but a strand of DNA which is contained inside a protein coat. Some viruses use RNA, but pupils do not need to know this at this stage. Viruses do not have a cell wall or a cell membrane. They can only replicate inside the cells of another organism, using them to make new viruses.

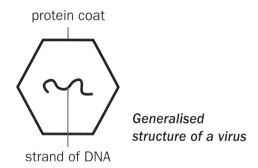

Generalised structure of a virus

Useful products produced by micro-organisms

Bacteria and fungi play an important role in the production of many foods and drinks, including yoghurt and cheese (for example, using lactic acid bacteria), bread and beer (using the yeast *Saccharomyces cerevisiae*).

Harmful diseases caused by micro-organisms

To cause illness, harmful micro-organisms have to enter the body and reproduce. The person is said to be infected. Bacteria and viruses cause disease by damaging the body's cells, tissues and organs, or by producing harmful chemicals called toxins.

Diseases caused by bacteria include tuberculosis, pneumonia (lung diseases) and salmonella food poisoning (salmonellosis).

Viruses are responsible for AIDS (caused by HIV), mumps (a disease affecting the salivary glands), measles, colds and 'flu (influenza).

Fungi cause Athlete's foot and ringworm.

the journey ahead

During Key Stage 4, pupils will learn about both pathogenic and useful micro-organisms in much greater detail. They will study:

- how fungi, bacteria and viruses replicate inside the body
- how to culture bacteria, and work with them using aseptic technique
- how the body develops immunity to micro-organisms
- mechanisms for avoiding the transfer of pathogens (introduced in *chapter 10: staying healthy*)
- the process of fermentation, and its use in the manufacture of food and drink products.

teaching issues

Latin names in the media

Help pupils get used to the correct use of Latin names by getting them to collect and check examples of scientific names used in newspapers and magazines. Even the 'quality' newspapers find it difficult to stick to the rules for the use of italics and a capital letter for the first name only. Pin corrected versions on a notice board.

Vocabulary and use of language

Correct use of Latin names

Bacteria, viruses and fungi are normally referred to by their full Latin name the first time that the name appears in a text. After this a shortened form using the first letter of the first name is used. *Escherichia coli* has been such a popular experimental organism that it is universally recognised by its shortened form, *E. coli*. Some species of fungi are referred to by a common name such as baker's yeast (*Saccharomyces cerevisiae*). Latin names for organisms use a system of 'binomial nomenclature' (originally made popular by Linnaeus), by having two parts:

- the genus name, the group that contains all the most closely related species
- the species name, which makes the two name combination unique for that species.

The name is normally all in lowercase with the exception of the first letter of the genus name, which is uppercase. Pupils should be taught that, when they type the Latin name, it should be written in italics. As it is difficult to write in italics, standard procedure for hand written documents is to underline the name.

Latin names enable you to draw some conclusions about a species even if you have never seen it before. For example, a lactic acid bacterium commonly involved in yoghurt production is *Streptococcus thermophilus*:

- *Strepto* – tells you that the bacteria form a twisted chain of cells
- *coccus* – tells you that the bacterium is spherical
- *thermophilus* – tells you the species of the bacterium (the name literally means 'heat loving')

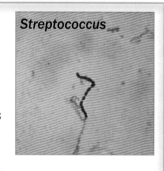
Streptococcus

For teachers only!

International codes are used to regulate the naming of organisms, to try to make sure that a species name is universal, no matter what language a scientist uses. Scientists meet together to ensure that no two species have the same name and that agreed classification groups are used.

Although the Latin name **Streptococcus thermophilus** *is in common use, this was first used in 1919. Since then, a better understanding of the group of closely related bacteria led to the official name changing to* **Streptococcus salivarius thermophilus**. *This indicates that there are closely related bacteria of the species Streptococcus salivarius of which this is the subspecies thermophilis. To be completely safe, the author's name and date can also be quoted when naming a species, here Orla-Jensen 1919 and Schleifer et al. 1995. L. or Linn. after the name show it was named by Linnaeus.*

Sizes of micro-organisms

Micro-organisms are so small that special units, micrometres (μm), are usually used to measure them. There are one thousand micrometres in a millimetre and one million in a metre. It is useful for pupils to have some idea of the size of micro-organisms, using real-world comparisons to make the sizes make sense. The diameter of a human hair, typically 0.1 mm or 100 μm can be used for this purpose.

organism	typical size	real-world comparison
fungi	5×10^{-6} m (5 μm)	20 fungal cells would fit across the diameter of a human hair
bacteria	1×10^{-6} m (1 μm)	100 bacteria would fit across the diameter of a human hair
viruses	1×10^{-7} m (0.1 μm)	1000 viruses would fit across the diameter of a human hair

Misconceptions

Misconception: All fungi are micro-organisms. Many pupils believe that all fungi are micro-organisms: living organisms which are too small to be seen without the aid of magnification. Mushrooms and toadstools are obviously not micro-organisms. They are made out of thread-like structures (hyphae) which can form solid structures that can be clearly seen by the naked eye.

Misconception: All micro-organisms reproduce by splitting and viruses are alive. Bacteria reproduce by growing in size and splitting in two (called binary fission). Yeasts, such as baker's or brewer's yeast, grow buds which split off when they are large enough to grow on their own. Viruses are quite unable to reproduce on their own and so are usually considered not to be 'living'. They release their DNA, with the genetic code to make new viruses, into host cells which become virus factories. Virus components are assembled into new viruses and released from the host cell, killing the cell and going on to infect new cells. Viruses therefore reproduce at a phenomenal rate - you can come down with the flu within a day or two of becoming infected.

Misconception: All micro-organisms are harmful. Many people refer to micro-organisms as germs, reinforcing the misconception that they are all harmful. Micro-organisms are essential in nutrient cycles, for example in recycling nitrogen by fixing it from the atmosphere or decomposing proteins in the dead remains and excreta of organisms. They have been used for centuries to make useful products such as bread and cheese. They are now widely used in the biotechnology industry to produce a vast range of products, including medicines. For example, genetically engineered bacteria are used in the production of insulin, used to treat people suffering from diabetes.

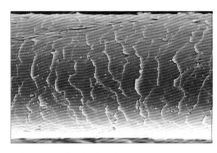

A scanning electron microscope image of a human hair

Comparisons with the width of a hair can help pupils to visualise how small micro-organisms are.

These fly agaric fungi are clearly not micro-organisms!

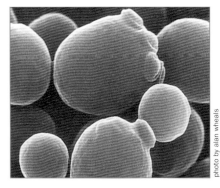

photo by alan wheals

This is the fungus Saccharomyces cerevisiae – also known as baker's or brewer's yeast. The 'bumps' on the cells are buds which grow and pinch off to form new cells.

Research opportunity

Ask pupils to research the use of micro-organisms in producing a useful product such as bread, beer, wine, yoghurts or cheese. Findings can be shared with the rest of the class through PowerPoint presentations.

Studying the growth of micro-organisms

Pupils could observe a range of microbial growth on agar plates. The presence of different coloured and shaped bacterial cultures means that several species are present on the plate. Fungal colonies tend to have a 'furry' appearance.

applications and implications

Scientists at work

Environmental Health Inspectors

Environmental Health Inspectors ensure that food premises and workplaces maintain a safe and healthy working environment. One of their functions is the investigation of complaints from people who have received unfit food, which may have caused food poisoning. Food poisoning is most often caused by bacterial contamination, due to insufficient hygiene procedures or inadequate storage or heating of food. Environmental Health Inspectors carry out a full investigation of the workplace following a complaint, and take appropriate action. In very serious cases, this can result in prosecution and the establishment being closed down.

Bread and beer

Yeast is used to ferment sugars. This is important in the production of beer and bread. Fermentation can be summarised by the equation:

sugar → ethanol + carbon dioxide

To make bread, flour, water and a small amount of sugar and yeast are mixed together. Yeast ferments the sugar, producing carbon dioxide. The bubbles of carbon dioxide cause the bread to rise. Ethanol, a form of alcohol, is also produced as an unwanted (waste) product, but this evaporates during cooking.

Beer is made from malted barley grains. Yeast is added to ferment maltose (a type of sugar) to make alcohol. During fermentation, carbon dioxide is the waste product.

Brewers

The process of making beer is known as brewing and takes place on an industrial scale in a brewery. All beers use fermentation of sugars in malted barley by yeast to produce alcohol. Most are then flavoured with hops (a flower), which gives beer its bitterness and acts as a natural preservative. Ales are made in a few days using fast acting top fermenting yeasts which leave behind some sugar residues and give a fruity flavour. Lagers are fermented for a month or more at a lower temperature. Slower acting bottom fermenting yeasts convert virtually all of the sugar into alcohol and carbon dioxide, leaving behind a clear, dry beer.

More sugar can be added for the yeast to ferment to increase the alcohol content. Yeast is often removed from a beer by filtration to make it clearer, though cask and some bottled beers retain yeast for secondary fermentation to add the 'fizz'.

Yoghurt and cheese

In yoghurt and cheese production, bacteria ferment milk sugars (for example, lactic acid bacteria convert lactose to lactic acid). This causes the protein in the milk to curdle and form into yoghurt or separate into curds and whey. In cheese making, an enzyme (rennet) is often added to help the process. The solid curds are separated from the liquid whey and pressed together to form cheese. 'Live' yoghurts are not pasteurised, and so contain the living bacteria which were used to make the yoghurt.

history and culture

Hooke's drawing of Mucor

He took his sample of mould from a leather book cover and saw what he thought were minute mushrooms - actually sporangiphores with sporangia.

Discovery of micro-organisms

The existence of micro-organisms was discovered in the seventeenth century by Robert Hooke and Antoni van Leeuwenhoek.

In his book *Micrographia* in 1665, Hooke published the first description of a micro-organism. Mycologists later identified the drawing as a picture of the microfungus Mucor – the common bread mould.

In 1675, Leeuwenhoek observed and described microscopic protozoa and bacteria. These important revelations were only made possible because of the ingenuity of Hooke and Leeuwenhoek in creating simple microscopes which could magnify objects from about 25 fold to 250 fold (though some think Leeuwenhoek achieved 600x).

Fermentation and decay

Before Leeuwenhoek's and Hooke's discoveries, it had been a mystery as to how grapes could be made into wine or why food went 'off'. Leeuwenhoek and Hooke did not make the connection between micro-organisms and these processes – their drawings only showed that these organisms existed. The connection was made by Lazzaro Spallanzani and Louis Pasteur.

These scientists ended the long-held belief that life could be spontaneously generated from non-living substances (normally during spoilage). For example, widely-held beliefs in the 18th century were that maggots were generated from rotting meat and flies from cow manure.

Spallanzani boiled broth in two separate bottles to kill off any organisms. He then sealed one bottle and left the other one open. A few days later, he could see the unsealed bottle had become turbid due to the activity of micro-organisms. The sealed bottle remained sterile, showing that spontaneous generation does not occur in the broth excluded from the air.

Pasteur designed bottles open to the air but with S-curved necks, so that gravity would prevent airborne materials reaching the boiled broth. Breaking the top off a bottle that had remained sterile for a year exposed the broth directly to the air, and within days it became turbid. From this he deduced that contamination came from life-forms in the air. Pasteur's work proved that the living organisms that grew in the broths came from outside, as spores in dust, rather than being spontaneously generated within the broth. He went on to devise the 'pasteurisation' process for wine, later used to make milk safe.

An illustration of Pasteur's S-necked bottle

Pupils could be asked to recreate Pasteur's experiments using test tubes and glass tubing.

Micro-organisms and disease

The first link between a bacterium and disease was made by Robert Koch in 1876. Koch carried out his research on the deadly disease anthrax, which affects farm animals and humans. He identified that the disease was caused by *Bacillus anthracis*, because the blood of cattle infected with anthrax always contained large numbers of this micro-organism. Koch found out that anthrax could be transmitted between animals by taking a blood sample from an infected animal and injecting it into a healthy one. He also discovered that he could grow *Bacillus anthracis* in a nutrient broth and inject it into a healthy animal to cause disease.

From these experiments, he devised his criteria for proving a specific micro-organism is the cause of a disease. These criteria are known as Koch's postulates:

- The micro-organism must be found in abundance in all organisms suffering from the disease, but not in healthy organisms.
- The micro-organism must be able to be isolated from a diseased organism, and grown in pure culture.
- The cultured micro-organism must cause disease when introduced into a healthy organism.
- The micro-organism must be re-isolated from the inoculated host, and identified as being identical to the original isolated micro-organism.

At the time, viruses could not be seen or cultured to meet all the criteria. Dmitri Iwanowsk is credited with discovering viruses in 1892, as agents that caused mosaic tobacco disease, but could pass through a filter that would trap all bacteria. It was not until 1930 that viruses were made visible by an electron microscope.

A colour-enhanced scanning electron micrograph of Bacillus anthracis (yellow), the cause of the disease anthrax in humans and livestock

Anthrax spores have also been used in biological warfare.

The red part is an erythrocyte (red blood cell).

hot topics

Feeding the masses?

During the 1950s, predictions of a global food shortage of protein-rich foods led to scientists carrying out research into a fungal-based food product, mycoprotein. In 1967, the fungus *Fusarium venenatum* was identified as the best candidate for making mycoprotein. The British government gave permission to sell mycoprotein for human consumption in 1980.

The fungus is grown in continuously oxygenated water, in sterile fermentation tanks. Glucose is added as a 'food' for the fungus. Vitamins and minerals are added to improve the nutritional value of the mycoprotein produced. Its texture is then altered so it resembles meat – it may be pressed into a mince or cut into chunks. It is high in vegetable protein and fibre, low in saturated fat and salt but contains lower levels of iron than most meats.

Mycoprotein and meat

Fusarium venenatum is a fungus used to make many meat-substitute products. Ask pupils to compare the advantages and disadvantages of eating mycoprotein instead of meat.

the journey so far

During Key Stage 2, pupils should have learnt that:

- to remain healthy, a person must eat a balanced diet
- exercise is important for maintaining a healthy heart and lungs
- drinking alcohol and smoking can damage a person's health
- doctors can sometimes prescribe medicines to help recovery from an illness.

All, either personally or through relatives and acquaintances, will have had experience of the effects of diseases of varying severity.

the science at key stage 3

To remain healthy, a person must eat a balanced diet (see *chapter 4*), exercise regularly (see *chapter 65*) and avoid taking harmful substances. There are also steps which can be taken to help prevent disease. If a person is infected, their white blood cells 'fight off' the disease (see *chapter 3*), though sometimes doctors have to intervene by prescribing antibiotics. Some diseases that are caused by micro-organisms can be prevented through immunisation.

Harmful substances

Drugs can be beneficial (have medicinal purposes) but all drugs, if misused, have the potential to cause harm. For example, they can cause liver damage, because this is the organ that breaks down drugs in the body. Drugs include:

- Depressants slow down the nervous system and the body's reactions. Examples include solvents, alcohol and cannabis.
- Stimulants speed up the nervous system and can make a person feel more energetic and alert. They can also cause insomnia, headaches, nervousness and a loss of concentration. Examples include caffeine and ecstasy.

Smoking causes a large number of premature deaths each year by increasing the risk of lung cancer, bronchitis, emphysema (a type of lung disease) and heart disease. Tobacco smoke contains more than a thousand chemicals. Three harmful substances in tobacco are:

- Tar – contains chemicals which cause cancer.
- Nicotine – the addictive drug in tobacco that affects the nervous system, narrowing blood vessels and increasing blood pressure, causing the heart to beat faster and causing heart disease.
- Carbon monoxide – a poisonous gas that reduces the amount of oxygen the blood can carry by binding into red blood cells in the place of oxygen, causing the heart to work harder, leading to heart disease.

Many of the cells lining the windpipe have tiny hair-like structures called cilia. Other cells produce mucus which traps dirt and micro-organisms. The cilia keep the airways clean by sweeping mucus up the windpipe (trachea) to the throat, where it is swallowed. Smoke and tar from smoking paralyse the cilia so that the mucus flows into the lungs, making it difficult for a person to breathe and often causing infections leading to bronchitis. This mucus also causes the smoker to cough, damaging the lungs further.

Alcohol, even in small quantities, can change a person's behaviour – most feel relaxed and happy, but some become aggressive and depressed.

Alcoholic drinks contain the drug ethanol, a depressant.

Drinking alcohol regularly increases the amount needed to have the same effect on your body – you develop a tolerance to ethanol. Heavy drinking over long periods can cause stomach ulcers, heart disease, sclerosis of the liver, brain damage and cancers.

The spread of diseases caused by micro-organisms

Pathogens can enter the body through natural body openings, cuts in the skin or animal bites. A person is more likely to become unwell if large numbers of micro-organisms enter. The most common ways are through contact with an infected person, or by being exposed to unhygienic conditions.

how to prevent infectious diseases being spread from an infected person			
method of spread	how micro-organisms are transmitted	protection method	diseases spread by this mechanism
air	through coughs and sneezes – tiny drops of liquid are released into the air (droplet infection)	cover mouth and nose using a mask or handkerchief	colds and 'flu
touch	contagious diseases are spread by touching infected people or objects an infected person has touched	avoid touching infected people or contaminated objects; bacteria on the skin can be killed by antiseptics; bacteria on surfaces can be killed by disinfectants	mumps and chicken pox
body fluids	during sexual intercourse	use condoms	syphilis and chlamydia
blood	through cuts or sharing needles	cover wounds with plasters; use new sterilized needles	HIV and hepatitis

Immunisations

Immunisation can prevent a person from catching some diseases caused by bacteria and viruses. Usually, a vaccine is injected containing a dead or weakened version of the pathogen. This stimulates an immune response. White blood cells produce antibodies to the injected micro-organism. If the person is later exposed to the disease, antibodies are available immediately to destroy the micro-organisms, preventing the person from becoming ill. The person is said to have immunity to the disease. The incidence of childhood diseases in the UK, such as diphtheria and polio, has been dramatically reduced by the programme of childhood immunisations.

Treating diseases caused by bacteria

Antibiotics are drugs used by doctors to treat conditions caused by bacteria, such as food poisoning and chest infections. Some antibiotics stop the bacteria reproducing whereas others kill them.

the journey ahead

During Key Stage 4, pupils will learn about mechanisms for staying healthy in much greater detail. They will study how:

- haemoglobin in red blood cells transports oxygen around the body
- to culture bacteria and work with them using aseptic technique
- the body develops immunity to micro-organisms
- bacteria and viruses actually cause disease.

teaching issues

Vocabulary and use of language

Slang terminology

Many pupils will be able to name some drugs. However, they will not always use the correct name for a particular drug. The table below includes common recreational drugs and some of their slang names. The list is not exhaustive. Try putting this table on the board and filling in slang names as pupils suggest them. Make sure pupils are taught to use the correct scientific name!

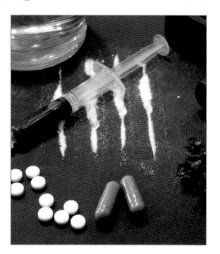

The dangers of drugs

As a research task, give pupils a copy of the drugs table and have them add another column to detail the dangers and long term effects of taking each drug.

---

drug and slang terms	short term effects
amphetamines speed; whiz	a group of stimulants which can cause euphoria, enhanced wakefulness, increased physical activity, decreased appetite, and feelings of power, strength, self-assertion, and enhanced motivation
cocaine charlie; coke	a powerfully addictive stimulant that directly affects the brain; it usually makes the user feel euphoric, energetic, talkative, and mentally alert
MDMA ecstasy; E	a stimulant and psychedelic drug; it produces an energising effect, as well as distortions in time and perception
heroin smack; gravy	a highly addictive drug; it is the most rapidly acting opiate resulting in profound relaxation and euphoria
LSD acid; tabs	a psychedelic drug which can produce delusions and visual hallucinations
cannabis / marijuana dope; grass	a psychoactive drug which can cause the user to feel happy and euphoric; colours and sounds may seem more intense, and time may appear to pass slowly

Dealing with sensitive issues

This topic will also be discussed in personal, social and health education (PSHE) lessons. Before teaching this topic, ensure you are familiar with your school's policy. Approach the topic from a scientific perspective, but be aware of the need for sensitivity to the personal circumstances of pupils and their families.

Misconceptions

Misconception: Smoking tobacco only causes lung cancer. Smoking increases the risk of many diseases. For example:

Chemicals in tar can cause cancer of the lung, mouth and throat. About a third of all deaths caused by cancer can be attributed to smoking.

Nicotine increases the risk of cardiovascular disease by increasing the heart rate, putting a strain on the heart and contributing to the build up of fatty deposits narrowing the arteries. This can lead to coronary heart disease.

Carbon monoxide increases the risk of cardiovascular disease by reducing the amount of oxygen that is carried in the blood making the circulatory system work harder. It also contributes to the build up of fatty deposits in the arteries.

Cigarette smoke kills ciliated cells, irritates the bronchial tubes and damages lung tissue. This can cause chronic bronchitis and emphysema.

Smoking also increases the risk of having a stroke.

Misconception: All drugs are harmful. Not all drugs are harmful. Some have very beneficial health effects when prescribed by a doctor or pharmacist and are taken according to the directions on the label. However, some drugs may still produce unpleasant side effects, even when used under medical guidance. Doctors have to weigh up the advantages and disadvantages of using each type of drug before they prescribe it to a patient.

Drugs can generally be considered harmful when their use causes physical, mental, social or economic problems. Illegal drugs are more likely to be hazardous. The effects of these drugs are much less predictable and potentially very dangerous.

Misconception: Antibiotics can be used to treat colds and 'flu. Antibiotics cannot treat viral diseases such as colds and 'flu – they do not harm viruses or fungi.

The range of drugs that doctors use in the treatment of diseases caused by micro-organisms are known as antimicrobial drugs. They work either by killing the micro-organism or by preventing the growth of a micro-organism.

Antimicrobial drugs can be divided into three categories:

1. Antibiotic drugs – used to treat bacterial infections.
2. Antiviral drugs – used to treat viral infections.
3. Antifungal drugs – used to treat fungal infections.

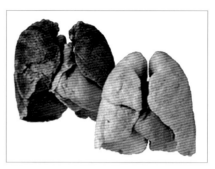

The photograph shows healthy human lungs (right) and lungs from a smoker (left). The blackening is caused by tar and smoke particles that contain chemicals which cause lung cancer. Approximately 90% of lung cancer victims are smokers.

Smoking-related disease

Smoking causes approximately 90% of deaths from lung cancer, 80% of deaths from COPD (chronic obstructive pulmonary disease), bronchitis and emphysema, and 15% of deaths from heart disease. Pupils could be asked to research one of the diseases caused by smoking. From their research they could produce a fact sheet about the disease to share with other members of the class. Pupils can find useful information on the Action On Smoking and Health website.

Cold and flu 'remedies'

People often buy 'over the counter medicines' to treat colds and flu. Many of these drugs contain both analgesic and anti-inflammatory components. These medicines do not actually cure the disease but help alleviate some of the symptoms. Pupils could be asked to find how these medicines treat the symptoms.

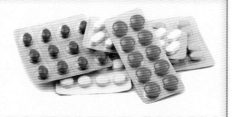

Misconception: Drugs are not addictive if they are only tried once. Drugs are chemicals which work by altering chemical reactions within the body. The body adjusts to these changes, so that normal function may become dependent on a drug. Absence of the drug causes withdrawal symptoms and the person is said to be addicted. These are often unpleasant and make it hard for a person to give up.

Addictiveness depends on the nature of the drug, its strength and the person taking it. Heroin is considered one of the most addictive drugs. It is possible to become addicted after just one dose.

Giving up smoking

Many people start smoking when they are at school, often as a result of peer pressure. In later life they may wish to give up smoking but find it very difficult to break their addiction. As a research activity, ask pupils to analyse the advantages and disadvantages of the various aids which people use to give up smoking, such as patches, sprays and chewing gum. Pupils can find useful information about giving up smoking on the NHS smokefree website.

applications and implications

Science at home

Use of detergents and disinfectants

People use a wide range of chemicals in their homes to help keep them clean and free from harmful micro-organisms. There are two main categories:

Detergents – these are chemicals intended to assist in cleaning. They contain a range of components depending on their precise job. For example, surfactants are added to dissolve grease, acids to dissolve lime scale and enzymes to digest proteins, fats and carbohydrates. They often have no effect on micro-organisms.

Disinfectants – these are antimicrobial agents which destroy or inhibit the growth of micro–organisms on non-living objects. Disinfectants should be distinguished from antibiotics (which destroy micro-organisms in the body), and antiseptics (which destroy micro-organisms present on living tissue). Methods of disinfection include the use of heat, radiation, or chemicals. Many disinfectants are toxic to humans and animals.

Cleaning products

Ask pupils to look through the cleaning products used to clean their own homes, or are available in their local supermarket. For each product they should state whether it is a detergent, a disinfectant or a mixture, and what it is used for.

Development of vaccines

Inoculation for smallpox became widespread in China in the sixteenth century. Powdered smallpox scabs were blown up the noses of healthy individuals. They mainly developed a mild case of the disease, but thereafter were immune to it. Although some became very ill and about 1 or 2% died, the treatment was considered worthwhile because of the 20-30% mortality rate of the disease itself. In the seventeenth century in Turkey, Persia and Africa, inoculation was carried out by adding scrapings from smallpox scabs to veins opened with a needle.

Edward Jenner, in 1796, developed a safe treatment against smallpox. He began his research after observing that dairymaids who caught the mild cowpox disease did not catch smallpox. He hypothesised that deliberately infecting a healthy person with cowpox would give them immunity from smallpox. In May, Jenner took matter from the fresh cowpox lesions on the hands and arms of Sarah Nelms, a young dairymaid, and inoculated it into James Phipps, an eight-year-old boy. Phipps developed a mild fever and discomfort in the glands in his armpits. Ten days later he was back to good health.

That July, Jenner took matter from a fresh smallpox lesion and inoculated Phipps again. He did not develop smallpox and Jenner concluded that the boy was now fully protected (immune) from the disease. Jenner invented the word 'vaccination' to describe his treatment, deriving it from the Latin vacca, meaning cow. Pasteur later adopted this term to describe the process of immunisation against any disease.

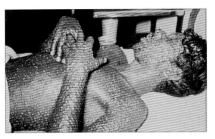

A smallpox sufferer

In 1980 the World Health Organisation declared smallpox an eradicated disease. A programme of vaccination, backed up by coordinated public health programmes across the globe succeeded in stamping out the disease.

Try asking pupils to sketch cartoons to illustrate the smallpox story.

> ### Ethical issues
>
> *Ask pupils: 'How ethical was Jenner's test on Phipps?'*

Discovery of penicillin

Penicillin was discovered by accident! In 1928, Alexander Fleming was investigating *Staphylococcus* bacteria growing on agar plates, when he noticed that a contaminating blue-green mould caused a zone of inhibition of bacterial growth. He grew a pure culture of the mould and found that it was a type of *Penicillium* (now known to be *Penicillium notatum*). He used the word 'penicillin' to describe an extract of broth cultures of the mould, which he found to be effective in killing bacteria. Numerous scientists worked on the drug, but it was many years before Florey and Chain devised an effective method to mass produce the drug. They shared the Nobel Prize for Medicine with Fleming in 1945.

Finding out about immunisation

Ask pupils:

'which diseases have you been immunised against?'

'why do you have to be immunised against some diseases more than once?'

'what are the advantages and disadvantages of immunisation?'

This can lead to a debate on whether they would give their own children an MMR immunisation.

hot topics

Binge drinking

Research into the drinking patterns of Europeans shows that drinkers in the UK may often be characterised as 'binge' or 'episodic drinkers'. On average, they drink less frequently than southern Europeans but, when they do, they consume more alcohol. In the UK, binge drinking accounts for 40% of all drinking occasions by men and 22% of those by women.

Social effects of binge drinking

Binge drinking is associated with increased levels of violence and the likelihood of being involved in an accident. Young people who participate in binge drinking are more likely to take part in risk-taking behaviours while drunk. These include going home with strangers, having unprotected sexual intercourse and taking part in 'pranks' which place themselves and others in physical danger.

Health effects of binge drinking

Excessive drinking is linked to many health problems, including:

- chronic diseases such as sclerosis of the liver
- cancers (especially liver, mouth, throat, larynx and oesophagus)
- injuries resulting from accidents
- sudden infant death syndrome (SIDS)
- alcohol dependence.

One unit of alcohol is equivalent to:

Most people are unaware of how much alcohol they are drinking. It takes approximately one hour for the body to break down one unit of alcohol.

half pint of normal strength beer or cider

small glass of wine

small glass of sherry

single measure of spirits

single measure of aperitifs

Drinking debate

Have pupils debate if 'happy hours' (when drinks are sold for heavily reduced prices, or the measures of drinks are increased) add to the problem of binge drinking. They could also discuss the effect of the 24 hour licensing laws (effective from 2005) from both a health and social perspective.

Antibiotic problems

Since the mass production of penicillin, bacterial infections have been treated with antibiotics, saving millions of lives worldwide. However, over-prescription (unnecessary use) has led to the appearance of many resistant strains of bacteria. Antibiotics can also cause problems by killing helpful bacteria in the body. They are a particular problem in hospitals, because seriously ill patients often have weakened immune systems.

MRSA and C. diff

Bacteria like methicillin-resistant *Staphylococcus aureus* (MRSA), *Clostridium difficile* (*C. diff*) and strains of tuberculosis have developed resistance to wide ranges of antibiotics. They are therefore very difficult to treat, and often fatal.

Antibiotics can disturb the normal bacterial balance of the body, especially in the gut. Many people have *Clostridium difficile* harmlessly present in their guts. Antibiotics may kill bacteria which have inhibited resistant C. diff, allowing it to grow and thus cause the death of weaker patients.

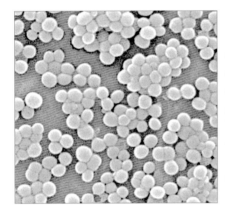

The spread of MRSA (illustrated) in hospitals caused nearly 1600 deaths in 2007. The spread of MRSA can be prevented through good hygiene practices such as washing hands thoroughly and keeping wounds covered. Ask pupils to write a hygiene protocol for nurses to follow to prevent MRSA being spread or ask them to research why MRSA is hard to control.

Shock campaigns

Leah Betts

Leah Betts died after taking just one MDMA (Ecstasy) tablet at her eighteenth birthday party. A photograph of Leah on her deathbed was released by her parents to try to shock other young people, and to stop them making the same mistake. As a result of her death, a short film – *Sorted* – was made, which was shown to approximately half a million children in the UK.

Anthony Hicks

Anthony Hicks, a 58 year old smoker, was the star of a hard hitting NHS advert targeting head and neck cancer, 90% of whose sufferers are smokers. Struggling to breathe, and with a visible hole in his throat following a laryngectomy operation, he talks about his illness and how his daughter is due to visit him from the USA. His final words are: "I will be alive to see that". The closing image states that he died ten days after filming, and never got to see his daughter.

Discussion

Have pupils discuss:

Do shock campaigns like this work?

What would they do to persuade people to stop smoking (or to never start)?

the journey so far

By the end of Key Stage 2, pupils should have learnt that:

- living things have many observable differences and similarities
- many living things can be grouped into 'plants' or 'animals' (and that animals include humans)
- keys can be used to identify different plants and animals.

They may have also learnt that:

- plants can be divided into flowering plants and non-flowering plants (and give examples)
- animals can be divided into vertebrates and invertebrates (and give examples)
- vertebrates can be divided into five smaller groups – mammals, birds, reptiles, amphibians and fish.

the science at key stage 3

Organisms are classified into different groups at different levels (known as taxonomic groups). All species within any group share certain characteristics. The system used today to classify organisms and to give each species a scientific name was developed by Carl Linneaus.

Keys can be used to allocate organisms to their groups, by systematically working through choices of observable features.

Five Kingdoms

Organisms are classified into five major groups, or kingdoms:

1. Plants: green plants such as trees and shrubs
2. Animals: such as mammals and insects
3. Fungi: mushrooms, moulds and yeasts
4. Protoctists: very simple organisms, including the animal-like protozoa, such as amoeba, and plant-like algae, such as seaweeds
5. Prokaryotes: bacteria and blue-green algae

Animal classification

The animal kingdom can be divided into two groups:

1. Vertebrates: animals with a backbone
2. Invertebrates: animals without a backbone

Vertebrate classification

Vertebrates can be divided into five classes:

1. Mammals: warm blooded; live young; hair
2. Birds: warm blooded; lay hard-shelled eggs; feathers
3. Fish: cold blooded; lay eggs in water; wet scales
4. Amphibians: cold blooded; lay soft-shelled eggs; moist skin
5. Reptiles: cold blooded; lay jelly-coated eggs in water; dry scales

Invertebrate classification

98% of all species are invertebrates. They are classified into more than 30 major groups (at phylum level).

Five are listed here:

1. Jellyfish (*Cnidaria*): tentacles; hollow bodies
2. Flatworms (*Platyhelminthes*): flat; thin bodies
3. Annelids: cylindrical bodies; segments.
4. Molluscs: usually have a shell; soft body; head and foot; no segments
5. Anthropods: hard exoskeleton; jointed legs

Plant classification

Plants can be divided into categories like this:

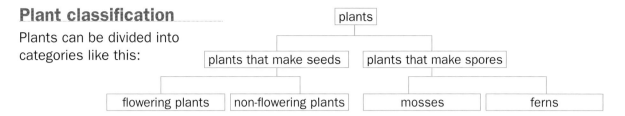

Variation within a species

Variation refers to the differences found in organisms. The characteristic differences which occur between species (interspecific variation) allow them to be distinguished and classified. Individual members of species also differ from each other (intraspecific variation). For example, humans vary in a number of characteristics including height, mass and hair colour. Variation within a species can be caused by factors which are inherited, environmental or a combination of both.

Continuous and discontinuous variation

Characteristics which have a range of values which can be measured on a numerical scale of units (an equal interval scale) show continuous variation. Examples include height and weight.

Characteristics which have no range, or contain discrete values falling into distinct categories show discontinuous variation. Examples include hair colour, eye colour and the ability to roll the tongue.

Inherited and environmental variation

In humans (and other organisms that reproduce sexually), offspring generally display some of their mother's and some of their father's characteristics, and sometimes a blend. This information is coded in DNA contained in genes, and passed onto the offspring via the sperm and egg cells (see *chapter 8*). Characteristics which show inherited variation include eye colour, gender and blood group.

Some variation within a species occurs as a direct result of factors in the environment to which an organism is exposed. Characteristics due to purely environmental factors include language spoken and presence of scars.

Some variation can be caused by a combination of inherited and environmental factors, for example hair colour (inherited colour altered by bleach or dye) and skin colour (affected by exposure to the Sun).

Selective breeding

Breeders can exploit the variation within a species by selective breeding. Only individuals which display a desired characteristic are used for breeding. The offspring produced are more likely to display this characteristic. Over many generations, the characteristic may build up. Modern dairy cattle produce more milk than their ancestors.

Scientists can use genetic engineering to insert the DNA of one species into another so it displays a desired characteristic. Bacteria, for example, are used to make human insulin to treat diabetes.

the journey ahead

During Key Stage 4, pupils will learn about variation and classification in much greater detail. They will study:

- how to classify an organism into its genus and species and use its scientific name
- how dominant and recessive genes determine which characteristic an offspring will display
- how to perform genetic crosses, and find the probability of a characteristic being inherited
- the advantages and disadvantages of selective breeding
- how an organism can be genetically engineered to display a specific characteristic.

teaching issues

Vocabulary and use of language

The five kingdoms

Linnaeus distinguished only two kingdoms – animals and plants. The need to separate out diverse organisms led to the widely accepted five, here referred to as animals, plants, fungi, protoctists and prokaryotes. The full Latinised names are Animalia, Plantae, Fungi, Protoctista and Prokaryotae (sometimes called Monera). The Protoctista kingdom came about when it was accepted that many multicellular organisms (such as seaweeds) were very closely related to single-celled organisms like Euglena and should be in the same kingdom. It is really a rag-bag of diverse organisms that cannot be fitted into the other groups, but are also difficult to split up into new kingdoms. It has been suggested that they should form twenty new kingdoms!

Organising nature

Originally, organisms tended to be grouped in lists according to their uses, for examples herbs according to their medicinal uses. By the eighteenth century, thousands of species had been identified and so there was a need for an organised system to name and categorise them.

Linnaeus' classification system aimed to accomplish three main goals:

1. To give each species a unique two-word name.

2. To distinguish between closely related species.

3. To organise groups of similar species into categories.

Linnaean classification has evolved to include seven main levels. Kingdom is the broadest category, with members sharing certain key major characteristics. Species is the most precise category, including organisms that can interbreed to produce offspring similar to themselves. Similar species that share certain characteristics can be grouped into a genus. Closely related genera can be grouped into families and so on.

At Key Stage 3, pupils should be familiar with kingdoms, the five vertebrate classes, and some examples of invertebrate phyla and species. Some pupils will be interested in using an organism's full Latin name and this should be encouraged.

Pupils should be able to use data or keys to classify a variety of organisms into their major groups.

The hierarchy of taxonomy

Species – Homo sapiens
▼
Genus – Homo
▼
Family – Hominidae
▼
Order – Primates
▼
Class – Mammalia
▼
Phylum – Chordata
▼
Kingdom – Animalia

Naming species

The system of naming species is known as binomial nomenclature. Each organism's Latinised name consists of two parts – the first indicates the genus name, the second indicates the species within that genus. Pupils should be taught that, when they name an organism using its Latin name, the word should be written in italics. (As it is difficult to write in italics, the standard procedure in hand written documents is to underline the name.) The name should be written in lowercase, with the exception of the first letter of the genus name which should be uppercase.

Looking at the domestic cat as an example:

Species – *Felis catus*

Genus – *Felis*

Family – *Felidae*

Order – Carnivores (*Carnivora*)

Class – Mammals (*Mammalia*)

Kingdom – Animals (*Animalia*)

Felis catus (left) and Felis silvestris (right) are close relations: same genus.

The domestic cat is given the unique scientific name *Felis catus*. *Felis* is the name of the genus to which the domestic cat belongs, *catus* denotes its species.

The wildcat, *Felis silvestris*, is very closely related to the domestic cat and therefore also belongs to the genus *Felis*.

The bobcat, *Lynx rufus,* and tiger, *Panthera tigris,* are sufficiently different from domestic cats and each other to belong to separate genera - *Lynx* and *Panthera*. However, all have the cat characteristics that allow them to be grouped together in the cat family, *Felidae*. Cats are also carnivores (order) and mammals (class).

Lynx rufus (left) and Panthera tigris (right) are not such close relations: different genera but same family.

Peer mentoring

Challenge gifted and talented pupils to choose a species of animal and explain the reasons why it is classified into its genus, family, order, class, phylum and kingdom.

Ask them to explain their findings to other individuals in the class as a form of peer mentoring.

The international system of classification is constantly being updated as new information is processed. The phylum Coelenterata is now defunct. The two former classes, Ctenophora (the 'comb jellies') and Cnidaria (includes 'true jellies') have been raised to phylum status.

Introducing classification

Before introducing pupils to the classification of living organisms, it is useful to relate the process to a situation with which they are more familiar. For example books in a library, food in a supermarket, or the various ways pupils are grouped within their own school.

Many pupils find the concept of classification easier to comprehend if they follow a 'hands on approach'. For example, pupils could sort a range of every day objects into groups, depending on the material they are made from. They could then take one of these groups and classify it further to demonstrate the hierarchical nature of taxonomy. As an example, glass objects could be sorted by colour.

Using keys

Pupils need to be able to use a variety of keys to classify organisms. They should be given the opportunity to use keys based on a series of paired statements, and branched keys. This will also allow them to become familiar with the biological names of groups.

Keys can be constructed by grouping specimens (or pictures) into groups by choosing two contrasting, visible characteristics at a time.

Paired statement key for garden invertebrates

1 legs – **go to 2**
   no legs – **go to 3**
2 six legs – **go to 4**
   eight legs – spider
3 shell – snail
   no shell – **go to 5**
4 coloured wings – butterfly
   colourless wings – fly
5 segments – earthworm
   no segments – slug

Branched key for garden invertebrates

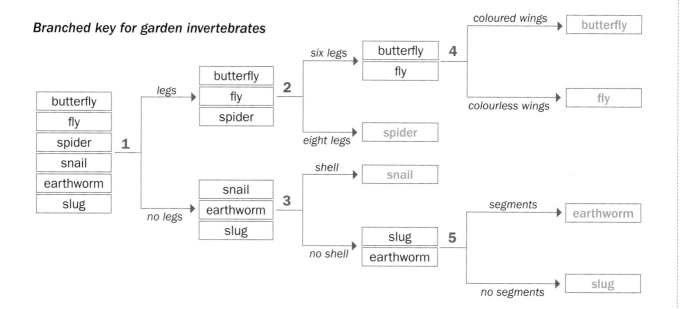

Design you own key

Challenge pupils to design their own key. For example, they could be asked to produce a key to identify a person's favourite sport or the name of a member of their class.

Continuous and discontinuous variation

Many pupils find it difficult to distinguish between continuous and discontinuous variation. Links can be made to the study of continuous and discontinuous data in maths, and how this data is displayed graphically. Discontinuous data is generally easier for pupils to understand, so this should be introduced first.

Graphical representation of a characteristic showing discontinuous variation

Characteristics which show discontinuous variation can be measured in a number of distinct categories. For example, a person can only have the blood type O, A, B or AB. They cannot have anything in between.

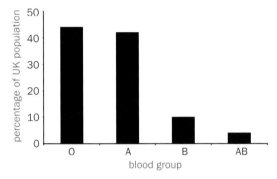

Discontinuous data is always displayed on a bar chart.

Graphical representation of a characteristic showing continuous variation

Within a population, characteristics which show continuous variation will display a range of measurements from one extreme to the other.

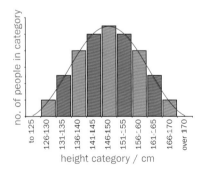

Continuous data is always plotted as a histogram. A line can be drawn on the chart to make it easier to see the shape of the graph. This type of variation produces a normal distribution curve – the mean, mode and median averages all have the same value.

Link between continuous/discontinuous variation and environmental/inherited variation

Discontinuous variation is controlled by the alleles (differing forms) of a gene or a very small number of genes. These characteristics generally, therefore, display inherited variation. The environment has little effect on these characteristics.

Continuous variation comes from the combined effect of many genes, and is often significantly affected by the environment. These characteristics are therefore usually a result of both inherited and environmental variation.

> **Class characteristics**
>
> *Ask pupils to gather data on a number of characteristics which can be measured within their class. They might measure hand span and height (continuous variation), eye colour and the ability to tongue roll (discontinuous variation). To help them decide whether these characteristics show continuous or discontinuous variation, ask pupils to plot their data in a graphical form. Pupils could also be asked to explain if the characteristics show inherited variation, environmental variation or a combination of both.*

Misconceptions

Misconception: Spiders are insects. Spiders (arachnids) and insects belong to the arthropod phylum, but can be distinguished at class level by the number of legs they possess. Other arthropod groups can be similarly distinguished:

1. insects – have six legs
2. arachnids – have eight legs
3. crustaceans – have between ten and fourteen legs
4. centipedes and millipedes – have more than twenty legs.

The jointed limbs are so adaptable that there are over a million identified arthropod species, most of which are insects.

Spiders have eight legs. They therefore belong to the arachnid group, not insects.

Misconception: Humans are not mammals or animals. Many pupils begin Key Stage 3 with the misconception that humans are not animals, but belong in their own group. Take pupils through each level of the hierarchy of classification step by step. This should make it clear that although humans are a distinct species, they share lots of features with other mammals and animals in general.

Misconception: All plants produce flowers. Pupils commonly believe that all plants produce flowers. This is probably because angiosperms (flowering plants) are the most widespread group of land plants and make up approximately 94% of all identified species. The remaining 6% do not produce flowers – these include the bryophytes (plants like mosses which reproduce using spores) and the gymnosperms (plants which reproduce using seeds but do not produce flowers). At this level, pupils should be familiar with the group of gymnosperms known as conifers and know that other groups exist.

Conifer seeds develop inside a protective cone. Normally when the cone reaches maturity, the scales open allowing the seeds to fall out and be dispersed by the wind.

History of classification

Attempts to systematically record plants date back to China in 2600 BC and records have been found on Egyptian papyri from the sevententh century BC. During the fourth Century BC, Aristotle distinguished the plant and animal kingdoms and grouped organisms in various ways through observations, for example by their means of transport – air, land, or water. He also used mode of reproduction and whether they contained red blood (roughly corresponds to vertebrates). A pupil, Theophrastus, is known as the father of botany from his work on plants, describing more than five hundred types and naming many groups still in use today.

In the first century AD, Pliny the Elder wrote a Natural History which tried to record everything known about the world and Dioscoroides wrote a volume on medicinal plants. These books were so influential, they were revered all through the dark ages. In 1583, Cesalpino produced the first important taxonomy of plants, using a hierarchical, graded order to arrange species. Malpighi expanded this hierarchical system to include animals. Subsequently, although attempts were made to distinguish and name organisms, especially useful plants, no real overriding system of classification was developed, and names were usually long Latin descriptions. The tomato was *Solanum caule inermi herbaceo, foliis pinnatis incisis* meaning 'smooth stemmed herbaceous solanum with incised pinnate leaves.' By the eighteenth century, the need to arrange species in taxonomies became paramount, due to the sheer number of species being recorded. Theophrastus identified five hundred plants, but by the late Renaissance John Ray had catalogued eighteen thousand.

Linnaeus set about classifying every living thing. Most attempts at taxonomies had started with large groups and sub-divided them, but Linnaeus worked in the opposite direction, grouping species by their similarities. He used Bauhin's system of nomenclature and developed Ray's ideas to distinguish six classes of animals: quadrupeds, birds, amphibians, fishes, insects, and worms. He enjoyed naming plants after people: the genus *Magnolia* after the botanist Magnol who he admired, but *Siegesbeckia*, an unattractive weed, after a critic Siegesbeck.

In his book *Systema Naturae* (1735), Carl Linnaeus introduced the system now referred to as Linnaean taxonomy. Linnaean taxonomy orders organisms into a hierarchy of groups based on an organism's physical characteristics. An organism's membership of a group demonstrates the characteristics it shares with other members. Although a number of changes to the system of classification have occurred since Linnean times, his system of naming and organising groups remains intact.

> **Three transport groups**
>
> *Challenge gifted and talented pupils to classify a number of animals into Aristotle's three 'transport' groups – air, land or water. Ask them to explain any problems they have encountered when using this system. Use examples such as: Where do you classify a duck? Is a fish really similar to a dolphin?*

Carl Linnaeus

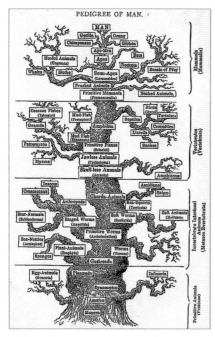

Ernst Haeckel's 'Tree of Life' – a first attempt to classify organisms on the basis of their phylogeny. This introduced the Protista as a third kingdom.

Developments in taxonomy

Changes take place constantly through the increasing understanding of the relationships between living things and through developments in technology, allowing us first to see detailed structure by using ever more powerful microscopes and, more recently, by studying genomes. One of the greatest changes in understanding has been the widespread acceptance of evolution as the mechanism of biological diversity and species formation. This resulted in the belief that classification systems should reflect how an organism has evolved over time (the phylogeny of an organism).

In 1969, Robert Whittaker proposed the five kingdom classification system, inspired by the need to separate the Fungi from the Plantae and to reorganise and divide the Protista. This system is described in this chapter and is favoured by European scientists.

In 1977, Carl Woese used molecular genetic analysis to propose a six kingdom classification by dividing bacteria into Eubacteria and Archaebacteria. This system is favoured by American scientists.

In 1990, Woese revised his previous system, using genome studies to propose a three-domain classification system: Bacteria, Archaea and Eukarya.

hot topics

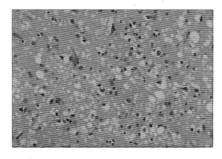

This photograph shows brain tissue from a person suffering with CJD. The pathological prion has caused holes in regions where brain cells normally communicate with each other. This prevents information being transferred, resulting in brain cell death and eventually the death of the patient.

Prions – another form of life?

Prions are infectious agents, made entirely of a mis-folded protein. Prions are thought to cause a variety of diseases including bovine spongiform encephalopathy (BSE or 'mad cow disease') and Creutzfeldt-Jakob disease (CJD) in humans. Prion diseases affect the structure of the brain or other neural tissue. These diseases are extremely rare but are currently untreatable, and therefore are always fatal.

Prions are not a new form of life as was originally believed. All mammals produce the prion protein (PrP) in their brains. However, this does not cause disease unless it has mutated. If mutant PrP gets into another mammal (for example, through eating the nervous tissue of an infected animal), contact is formed with 'normal' PrP. The mutant PrP can cause the normal PrP to change conformation, forming the disease-causing strain of prion.

Pupils often question why a comprehensive system of classification has not been developed. The following facts and figures could be used to explain some of the difficulties in coming up with a perfect system:

1. Approximately 1.5 million species of living organisms have been given a scientific name.

2. Each year approximately 13 000 new species are identified.

3. It has been estimated that approximately two thirds of all living species are insects.

4. Most scientists believe that up to 10 million species of living organisms exist. However, there have been estimates that up to 100 million exist.

5. The palaeontologist Steven Jay Gould estimated that 99% of all plant and animal species that have existed have already become extinct and most have not left any fossils.

6. Only about 1% of all animal species are larger than a bumble bee.

the journey so far

During Key Stage 2, pupils should have learnt:
- that plants need air, light, water, warmth and nutrients to grow
- that seeds need warmth to germinate
- the function of the roots, stem and leaves
- the names and functions of parts of the flower
- the stages in the life cycle of a flowering plant
- some differences between insect- and wind-pollinated flowers.

the science at key stage 3

Plants are producers. They make their own food by the process of photosynthesis, using the energy of sunlight that has been absorbed by chlorophyll. Chlorophyll is the pigment that gives leaves and some stems their green colour. Energy used to make food in plants becomes available to consumers that cannot make their own food.

Photosynthesis

Photosynthesis is a chemical reaction which takes place in plants. Plants use energy in sunlight to convert carbon dioxide and water into glucose and oxygen. Glucose is a simple sugar which can be used for growth, resulting in increased biomass. Some glucose is also converted into starch and stored until required.

Photosynthesis equations

The process of photosynthesis can be represented in the following word and chemical equations:

$$\text{carbon dioxide} + \text{water} \xrightarrow{\text{light energy}} \text{oxygen} + \text{glucose}$$

$$6CO_2 + 6H_2O \longrightarrow 6O_2 + C_6H_{12}O_6$$

Photosynthesis occurs in the chloroplasts found in certain plant cells. This predominantly occurs in palisade tissue in the leaves, but some photosynthesis also occurs in stems (if green).

Movement of the reactants and products of photosynthesis

light energy from the Sun is trapped in chlorophyll inside chloroplasts

carbon dioxide enters and oxygen leaves by diffusion through stomata (tiny holes)

water and sugars are transported throughout the plant – water in xylem vessels, sugars in phloem vessels

water is absorbed into plant roots from the soil; tiny hairs cover the roots, increasing the surface area

Factors affecting the rate of photosynthesis

Four factors affect the rate of photosynthesis: light intensity (the higher the light intensity, the faster the rate); carbon dioxide concentration (the higher the concentration, the faster the rate); availability of water (lack of water slows down photosynthesis and causes wilting or loss of leaves); surrounding temperature (the optimum temperature for most land plants is approximately 30 °C).

Stages in the life cycle of a plant

Plant life cycles involve growth and ...

Germination
To germinate and begin to sprout and grow into a seedling, a seed needs oxygen, water and warmth.
Pollination
Pollination is the transfer of pollen from an anther to a stigma in a different plant (cross-pollination) or in the same plant (self-pollination). There are two types of flower. They use different mechanisms to transfer pollen: (1) Insect pollinated flowers make small amounts of very sticky pollen in large, brightly coloured, sweet smelling flowers that have nectar to attract insects. Stamens and carpels are inside so insects brush against them.   (2) Wind pollinated flowers tend to be dull, small flowers with no scent. Pollen is produced in large quantities and is very light. The stamens and carpels hang outside the flowers to release and catch drifting pollen.
Fertilisation
Pollen landing on a suitable stigma (normally the same species), grows a pollen tube down the style into an ovule in the ovary. Fertilisation occurs when the pollen grain nucleus travels down the tube and joins with the nucleus of the ovule. The ovary will develop into the fruit and the ovules will become seeds.
Seed and fruit dispersal
There are two main types of seeds or fruits: (1) Wind dispersed seeds and fruits such as dandelion seed 'parachutes' and sycamore 'keys'. (2) Animal dispersed seeds and fruits such as tomato or blackberry are eaten and dispersed in droppings; others, such as burdock, have hooks and are trapped in animal fur. Some plants, such as gorse, use explosive mechanisms. Some, such as pond iris, use water.

Plant mineral requirements

To remain healthy, plants need to absorb minerals such as nitrogen (N), phosphorous (P) and potassium (K) from the soil. They are used with the glucose from photosynthesis to make other molecules, including proteins. Soils which contain sufficient amounts of these minerals are said to be fertile. They may be added to infertile soils in manure or fertilisers. Fertilisers containing these three key nutrients are often referred to as NPK fertilisers.

the journey ahead

During Key Stage 4, pupils will learn about plants in much greater detail. They will study:

- the process of photosynthesis in more detail
- how water is absorbed into the roots by the process of osmosis
- how guard cells open and close stomata
- how to identify which mineral deficiency a plant has, based on its appearance.

teaching issues

Rate of photosynthesis

Rate of photosynthesis can be measured by collecting oxygen released from pond weed such as Elodea. The simplest method is to count the number of bubbles released from a cut stem in a given time. The effect of changing light intensity can be easily demonstrated, by moving a lamp away from the plant, causing a fall in the rate of gas production. (Light intensity varies by the inverse square law, doubling the distance reduces the light by a quarter, halving it increases it by four times.)

Key term definitions

Key terms could form solutions to crossword clues, terms in a word search or anagram puzzles. Fun approaches to learning key terms aid pupils' memory and enthusiasm.

When to teach this topic

There is a range of practical work which can be used to teach this topic. It is, therefore, sensible to timetable the teaching of plant-based topics into the spring or summer months, when plants are actively photosynthesising and growing at a faster rate.

It is also important to remember that some experiments take long periods to complete. Investigating how the absence of light affects photosynthesis by analysing starch production, for example, requires plants to be kept in the dark at least overnight before testing. Growth experiments, to see the effect of nutrient deprivation for example, may take weeks. It is essential that these experiments are effectively pre-planned to fit into a sequence of lessons that allow sufficient time for the experiments to yield meaningful data.

Vocabulary and use of language

Key terms

There are a number of important definitions of key terms within this topic. These include photosynthesis, germination, pollination and fertilisation. Pupils should be encouraged to use these words throughout their work during this topic. Pupil's learning and retention of the key terms is enhanced when a variety of approaches is used. For example, pupils could be asked to come up with their own definitions for each of the key terms. They could then share these with a partner, and amend them as a pair. This definition can then be shared with small groups and eventually with the class. This will help pupils to recall these key terms, as they will have a sense of ownership over the definitions. Pupils also need to have a working knowledge of the parts of a flower. More able pupils should be able to use the correct scientific names.

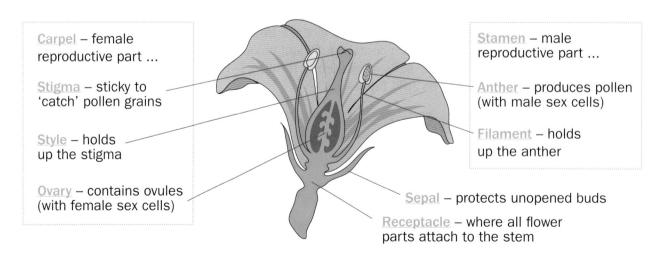

Carpel – female reproductive part …

Stigma – sticky to 'catch' pollen grains

Style – holds up the stigma

Ovary – contains ovules (with female sex cells)

Stamen – male reproductive part …

Anther – produces pollen (with male sex cells)

Filament – holds up the anther

Sepal – protects unopened buds

Receptacle – where all flower parts attach to the stem

Photosynthesis equation

At Key Stage 3, only the word equation for photosynthesis is required. However, the most able pupils find the balanced chemical equation satisfying, as it explains more fully what happens to the reactants. Light energy is usually written above the arrow between the reactants and products, as without this energy, the reaction cannot take place.

The photosynthesis equation is virtually a 'reversal' of the respiration equation. Consequently, many pupils tend to mix up the two equations. This does allow the opportunity, however, of exploring the relationship between the Animal and Plant kingdoms.

Misconceptions

Misconception: Plant cells do not respire. Plant cells are constantly respiring in the same way as animal cells. If plants stop respiring they will die, because they need energy for living processes. The idea that plants do not respire is associated with two different misconceptions. Some pupils believe that plants photosynthesise, whereas animals respire. Other pupils believe that respiration is the same as breathing, and therefore plants cannot carry out this process.

Take opportunities to distinguish breathing and respiration. Emphasise that plants cannot breathe but respire all the time.

Misconception: Plants only photosynthesise during the day and only respire at night. It is important that pupils understand that plants can only photosynthesise in the light. So plants can only photosynthesise during the day, but not during the hours of darkness. Hence they release oxygen in daylight and carbon dioxide in the dark. This easily leads to the misconception that plants only respire at night.

Ensure that pupils understand that plants are respiring and making carbon dioxide all the time. In daylight, the carbon dioxide they produce is used up in photosynthesis.

Misconception: Plants photosynthesise all year round. Deciduous plants lose their leaves in winter and therefore are unable to photosynthesise for several months of the year. These plants store enough food produced during the summer by photosynthesis to last them over winter, and to provide energy reserves for new growth in the spring.

Misconception: Plants can't photosynthesise in winter. Evergreen plants do not lose their leaves, so are able to photosynthesise all year round. However, reduced sunlight and low temperatures may greatly reduce the rate of growth. Once again, it is worth reinforcing that plants can only photosynthesise in the light (see above) while avoiding the misconception that plants only photosynthesise during the day and only respire at night.

This is a deciduous tree. It does not carry out photosynthesis during the winter months but survives from food stores produced in the summer months through photosynthesis. It will begin to photosynthesise again in the spring, when new leaves form.

Misconception: Seeds need light to germinate. Many pupils believe that seeds need light to germinate, because plants need light to grow. A seed only requires oxygen, water and heat to germinate, because it is using energy stored in the seed to grow. The temperature required to initiate germination varies between species. Normally after a few days, the new seedling will produce leaves and begin to photosynthesise. It now requires light.

Misconception: Plants obtain their food from the soil. Many pupils believe that plants get their food from the soil – that soil is 'plant food'. Such pupils find this a difficult misconception to overcome, but it can be addressed in a number of ways:

- Show pupils plants which grow in water (for example, *Elodea*, pictured), or 'air plants' (for example, *Tillandsia*) to demonstrate that not all plants live in soil.

- Plants which grow in soil can be demonstrated to grow normally in a mineral solution. Basil plants are effective for this demonstration. This method of propagation is known as hydroponics.

- Put a healthy plant, which is growing in soil, into the dark for a long period of time. Show pupils that it will grow abnormally and eventually die if it does not have light to produce its own food, even though it is in a rich soil. This can be linked to grass being killed, for example, if covered by a tent during a family holiday.

Misconception: All plants have flowers. See the misconceptions section in *chapter 11: variation and classification*.

applications and implications

Science at Work

Hydroponics

Hydroponics is the name given to the technique of growing plants in nutrient solutions (water and minerals), without the use of soil. In temperate regions of the world, all hydroponic systems are located in greenhouse-type structures which enable the temperature to be controlled, reduce the amount of water loss through evaporation and reduce disease and pest infestations. This method also allows plants to be grown out of season and requires far less land than traditional farming techniques. Disadvantages of a hydroponic growing system include high capital costs and the high degree of management of the system required for success.

Most tomatoes grown commercially are produced using hydroponic systems. This system allows many crops to be grown all year round, even in cooler northern climates such as the UK.

Use of bees in greenhouses

Many crops are grown in greenhouses in the UK. A major disadvantage of growing crops indoors is the exclusion of insects – bees in particular – which naturally cross-pollinate plants, leading to the production of fruit. An industry has grown up rearing bees for use in these environments. Commercial greenhouses require bees all year round to satisfy the demand for produce.

Bumble bees, rather than honey bees, are reared for this purpose. Bumble bees are particularly efficient at pollinating plants.

Bumble bees pollinate most tomatoes grown in commercial greenhouses. They pollinate the tomato plant by a process known as 'buzz pollination'. The bumble bee grabs the anther and shakes it, releasing pollen (that would otherwise stay trapped), which is then available to fertilise flowers resulting in fruit production. Good pollination produces large, evenly shaped fruits.

Why bees?

Encouraging bees into gardens is essential for ensuring that plants are pollinated so that fruits are produced. Ask pupils to design a leaflet which contains useful tips to encourage bees into their own gardens.

history and culture

Scientific understanding of photosynthesis

Photosynthesis is a vitally important process responsible for feeding the majority of living organisms on Earth. It also produces the oxygen required by animals to survive. Yet a basic understanding of photosynthesis was hard to establish. A number of scientists working in different countries were involved, each making a contribution through observation and experiment.

In the mid seventeenth century, Jan van Helmont measured the mass of a willow tree growing in a pot and the mass of the soil in which it was growing. Although the mass of the plant increased by 74kg, there was very little change in the mass of the soil. From these observations he proposed that most of the mass of the growing plant must come from the water that he added, rather than from the soil.

Try it yourself

Pupils could be asked to choose one of the famous experiments which helped in the discovery of photosynthesis. They could then carry out the experiment itself and write a report explaining which part of the photosynthesis equation the experiment helped to prove.

Gifted and talented pupils might be asked to research the phlogiston theory. Challenge them to explain why this was so difficult to overcome.

Joseph
Priestly

Jan Ingenhousz

In the late seventeenth century John Woodward designed some experiments to test Helmont's hypothesis. In his experiments, he observed that a plant only increased in biomass by a very small amount, despite several thousand times more mass of water being added. These experiments resulted in Helmont's hypothesis being dismissed. Woodward correctly hypothesised that most of the water escaped from the plants pores into the atmosphere.

Joseph Priestly in the 1770s carried out two important experiments when studying the composition of air:

1. He burnt a candle in a bell jar containing a fixed amount of air. He observed that the candle burnt out a long time before it ran out of wax. He then repeated the experiment with a sprig of mint in the jar. The candle initially burnt out, but he managed to relight it 27 days later (by focusing a sunlight beam).

2. He kept a mouse in a transparent container containing a fixed amount of air. The mouse died. He repeated this experiment, but this time placed a plant in the jar and found that the mouse survived.

These two experiments proved that plants change the composition of air. Priestley hypothesised that plants restore to the air whatever substances breathing animals or burning candles remove.

At around the same time, in 1778, Jan Ingenhousz placed an unlit candle and a plant inside a transparent sealed container. He placed the apparatus in sunlight, and left it for a few days. He then covered the apparatus with a dark cloth for several days. The candle would not light. This research led him to conclude that in the dark, the plant must have respired, fouling the air (which is incorrect) and that plants need light to purify or 'revitalise' the air.

Ingenhousz also exposed aquatic plants to bright sunlight and observed gas bubbles forming around the leaves and green parts of the stems. Ingenhousz concluded that it must be what the plant produces that purifies air fouled by animals or candles. When the plants were observed in darkness, the bubbles stopped.

Ingenhousz was able to show that the amount of oxygen released during photosynthesis is greater than that absorbed in respiration. He suggested that green plants take in carbon dioxide and release oxygen. This was later demonstrated in 1796 by Jean Senebier. Senebier also demonstrated that photosynthesis does not occur in boiled water from which the gases have been excluded. Sources disagree as to whether Ingenhousz or Senebier showed that it was the light and not the warmth of sunlight that was necessary for photosynthesis to occur.

These observations and experiments established that plants needed their green parts and light to take up carbon dioxide and release oxygen, suggesting that the oxygen is produced from the breakdown of carbon dioxide. Water had also been ruled out of the equation.

A few years later Nicolas-Theodore de Saussure demonstrated that the increase in biomass of plants must be a result of the uptake of carbon dioxide and water. He enclosed plants in glass containers, and weighed both the plants and enclosed carbon dioxide over a period of time. He showed that:

- plants absorb carbon dioxide during photosynthesis
- carbon in plants comes from the atmosphere not the soil
- the volume of carbon dioxide absorbed is approximately equal to the volume of oxygen produced
- the mass of carbon absorbed was less than the total increase in mass of the plant

De Saussure reasoned that the missing mass is made up by water being absorbed and used in photosynthesis. This led to the major chemical transformations in photosynthesis being identified and the basic reaction of photosynthesis being derived:

$$carbon\ dixoide\ +\ water\ \xrightarrow{\text{light energy}}\ oxygen\ +\ glucose$$

Despite this knowledge being established in the 1800s, it was not until the 1940s that Samuel Rubin used the 'heavy' oxygen isotope (^{18}O) to show that the oxygen came from water and not from carbon dioxide.

Splitting water

Challenge pupils to show how using ^{18}O as a label (in water or carbon dioxide) can be used to prove that oxygen is produced in photosynthesis by 'splitting' water and not carbon dioxide. Rubin used a mass spectrometer to distinguish atomic masses. He found no oxygen released during photosynthesis by a plant given labelled carbon dioxide ($C^{18}O_2$), but it was present when the plant was given labelled water ($H_2^{18}O$).

history and culture

Colourful flowers

Some florists sell flowers that have been artificially dyed to enhance their colour. By placing the flower stems in coloured dye, the flowers draw up the water through the xylem vessels in their stems. The coloured dye then spreads throughout the plant resulting in a different coloured, or a more vibrantly coloured, flower.

Vegetarianism

Plants make all the nutrients they need and herbivores get all the nutrients they need from a vegetarian diet. So, why do humans eat meat? Challenge pupils to form teams for and against vegetarianism. They could research and collate evidence to put forward a case for their side of the argument. Arguments could be put forward in debate, on posters or in PowerPoint presentations.

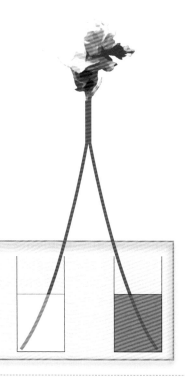

Split carnations

Split the stem of a white carnation. Place half of it in a glass of coloured water. Put the other half in a plain glass of water. Over time, the corresponding half of the carnation will change colour. Pupils could carry out similar experiments.

the journey so far

During Key Stage 2, pupils should have learnt:

*   plants and animals live in different habitats
*   how some plants and animals are suited to the environment of their habitat
*   plants and animals are linked in food chains
*   plants are producers and animals are consumers
*   producers are located at the start of a food chain
*   the difference between predators and prey.

the science at key stage 3

Habitats and the environment

A habitat is the place in which an organism lives. Examples of habitats include desert, meadow, forest and pond. Each has its own set of distinguishing features. The environment is an organism's surroundings, including the range of conditions found there, such as the temperature and water availability.

Adaptations

Organisms survive because they are adapted to the environment in which they live. They have to compete for resources, such as food, water and space with other organisms living in the same habitat.

Polar bears have adapted to live in the harsh polar environment of the Arctic. They are so well insulated they are hardly visible using infra-red photography.

*   Thick layers of fat (up to 10 cm) and fur for insulation.
*   White fur for camouflage.
*   Large hairy feet that reduce pressure, for walking on snow and ice, and prevent slipping.

Cacti have adapted to survive the extreme heat and arid conditions found in a desert.

*   Thick waxy coating to prevent water loss by evaporation.
*   Spines (modified leaves) lose very little water through evaporation and protect against predators.
*   Stem carries out photosynthesis, instead of leaves, and stores water.

Changing environments

Adaptations are necessary to cope with changes in environmental conditions in habitats. Daily changes include light levels and temperature. Seasonal changes include colder winters with shorter days. Hence most animals, apart from nocturnal hunters such as owls and their prey, tend to sleep at night. Many plants are dormant or slow growing in winter – many lose their leaves – so there is less vegetation available for food. Many animals store up fat in the summer to use for food and insulation in the winter. Some hibernate.

Seashore intertidal zones support a variety of plants and animals adapted to different periods of exposure to the air. For example, when submerged, barnacles feed (by sticking out their legs!) and limpets move over the surface of the rock, eating algae. When the tide goes out, barnacles close up and limpets cling tightly to the rock. This helps to prevent them losing water and being eaten by predators.

Feeding relationships

Feeding relationships of organisms in a particular habitat can be shown in a food chain or food web.

Food chains and food webs

Arrows in food chains show how energy flows from one organism to another as they eat and are eaten. Many different terms are used to describe feeding relationships, for example humans are omnivores: we eat both plants and animals. Most species have more than one source of food, so food chains may be interlinked to show food webs.

Relationships in a food chain:

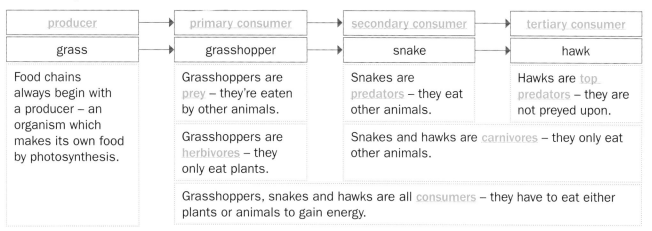

producer	primary consumer	secondary consumer	tertiary consumer
grass	grasshopper	snake	hawk
Food chains always begin with a producer – an organism which makes its own food by photosynthesis.	Grasshoppers are prey – they're eaten by other animals.	Snakes are predators – they eat other animals.	Hawks are top predators – they are not preyed upon.
	Grasshoppers are herbivores – they only eat plants.	Snakes and hawks are carnivores – they only eat other animals.	
	Grasshoppers, snakes and hawks are all consumers – they have to eat either plants or animals to gain energy.		

Pyramids of numbers

A pyramid of numbers can be used to show the populations (number of each organism) in food chains living in a habitat. As the source of food, the producer always goes at the start of a food chain and the bottom of a pyramid. The length of each bar is proportional to the number of individuals at each feeding (trophic) level.

Energy is transferred into the environment as it is moved from one level to the next. It is removed from organisms in such things as droppings and lost leaves, and as heat. The size of organisms also generally increases. Therefore there are fewer and fewer organisms at each level.

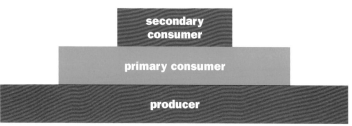

the journey ahead

During Key Stage 4, pupils will learn about the environment in greater detail. They will study:

- pyramids of biomass as a way of displaying feeding relationships
- how to interpret food webs in more detail
- the use of biological control in controlling pest populations
- the impact of humans on the environment.

teaching issues

Vocabulary and use of language

Some pupils may have done a substantial amount of work on environmental issues, possibly involving projects, visits and fieldwork. They will already have a vocabulary of specialist terms, but may lack confidence in their use or confuse terms like environment and habitat.

Key Terms

This topic is full of key terms. These include producer, consumer, herbivore, carnivore and omnivore. Pupils should be encouraged to use these words whenever they are referring to a feeding relationship. The more practise pupils have at using these words, the more confident they will become.

An example food web:

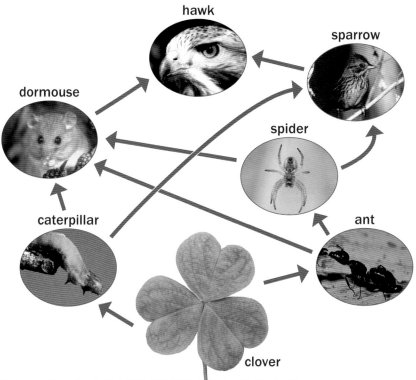

Pupils can work in small groups to create their own food webs using species cards which can be stuck in place to form posters. Groups can compare and criticise or support the feeding relationships identified. If they have investigated a habitat at first hand, pupils can create their own cards using the organisms they have found.

Ask pupils to write out the terms they should know, such as consumer, herbivore or prey, then attach them to appropriate organisms.

Identifying adaptations

Pupils should be able to identify and describe adaptations of animals and plants living in a variety of different habitats. Many have difficulties working out such adaptations, but find it easy to identify what is wrong in very badly adapted made up organisms. For example, a bald, very fat purple camel with no hump that walks on tip-toes gives clues to the adaptations needed to live successfully in a desert environment.

Camels have adapted to survive hot, dry, desert conditions. Ask pupils to design an organism which is adapted to survive in an environment of their choice. The organism can be unrealistic, provided its features display characteristics which would enable it to survive the chosen habitat.

Teaching food chains and webs

Drawing arrows

Many pupils have difficulty using arrows in the correct direction to show energy flow in food chains and webs – their diagrams, for example, might show that grass eats cows. Pupils who are unsure can have difficulties answering questions about food webs, especially if they are unfamiliar with the animals in question.

Give pupils lots of practice in drawing their own food chains and webs to ensure they are confident in adding arrows pointing in the correct direction. Ideally, they can use organisms they have identified themselves, in field work or from posters showing organisms in contrasting habitats. Provide secondary data for unfamiliar organisms to assist the recognition of potential feeding patterns.

At the time of writing, cards for 140 plants and animals, with name, food chain information and a brief description can be found on the website of the Royal Botanical Gardens, Kew.

Matching habitats

Reinforce ideas about adaptations by asking pupils to match pictures of animals and plants to a range of habitats. Ask them to select what they think are the most important adaptations of the organisms to the suggested habitats. Challenge them to justify their choices in class discussions.

Science club / Data logging

Challenge pupils to investigate how animals and plants are adapted to changes over a 24 hour period. Ask them to hypothesise about expected change and the reasons for them. If available, use data logging equipment with temperature, light and sound probes or automatic weather stations. If your school has CCTV equipment, see if this can be used to monitor nocturnal animals such as urban foxes.

Demonstrating food chains

Provide pupils, in small groups, with cards containing the names of a plant, a herbivore, and a carnivore, plus two arrows. Ask each to take a card and organise themselves into the correct order, with the arrows pointing in the correct direction.

This can be used to introduce food webs: if the same animals and plants are used in different combinations, pupils will notice that the same organisms can be found in different chains.

The 'web of life' game

Produce large cards naming the animals and plants in a food web. Attach a card to each pupil and ask them to sit in a circle, with a pupil to represent the Sun in the middle. Pass wool or string between pupils to represent the energy transfer between organisms. Many situations can be studied by using this model. To represent death, pupils could let their piece of thread hang loose. What would happen if all the green plants died, or a particular organism got a disease which killed them all? Anyone who is touching this thread would therefore be directly affected.

All energy comes from the Sun

Pupils should be constantly reminded that the energy within a food chain comes from the Sun. It is important to emphasise that without the Sun, producers would not be able to produce glucose and other food molecules which they need to grow and reproduce, which are in turn passed onto animals. One way of reinforcing this is to ask pupils to add the Sun to the start of each food chain.

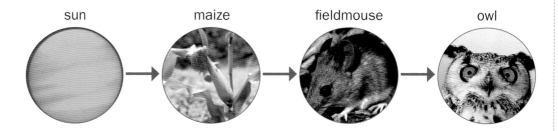

Teaching pyramids of numbers

The pyramid shape

Generally, pyramids of numbers are pyramid shaped because a larger number of smaller organisms is needed to support a smaller population of larger organisms.

A pyramid of numbers for a cabbage field.

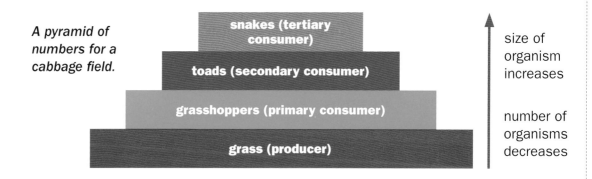

Pupils can produce accurate pyramids of numbers by drawing them on graph paper. They need to select an appropriate scale to represent all the organisms.

Unusually shaped pyramids of numbers

'Pyramid of numbers' implies that the number of organisms present in a particular habitat always decreases between trophic levels. However, a variety of shapes can be produced and pupils should be exposed to situations in which this occurs.

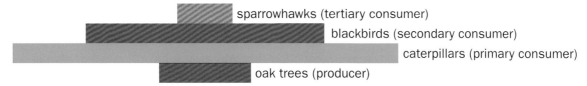

sparrowhawks (tertiary consumer)

blackbirds (secondary consumer)

caterpillars (primary consumer)

oak trees (producer)

Large producers can feed many small consumers, giving a small base to the 'pyramid'. A single oak tree is far larger than a grass plant and will produce an inverted pyramid of numbers.

fleas (tertiary consumer)

foxes (secondary consumer)

rabbits (primary consumer)

grass (producer)

Pyramids of numbers also become distorted when small parasitic organisms, such as fleas or ticks, are included. One cat or fox, for instance, can provide a home for hundreds of fleas.

Pyramids of biomass

The biomass, or total amount of the living material in organisms at each trophic level, can be estimated (usually as dry mass, to exclude water) and plotted as bars in a pyramid. Pyramids of biomass are not inverted if they show average values over a whole year. Seasonal fluctuations can cause inversion: biomass of animal plankton in the English Channel can exceed that of the plant plankton food source in the autumn. Photosynthesis slows and the tiny algae are eaten more rapidly than they grow.

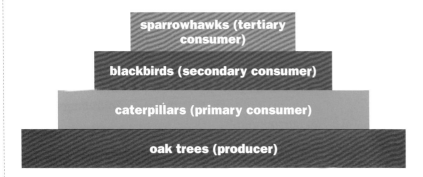

sparrowhawks (tertiary consumer)

blackbirds (secondary consumer)

caterpillars (primary consumer)

oak trees (producer)

An oak tree pyramid of biomass. Compare it with the corresponding pyramid of numbers above.

(not to scale)

Biomass v Numbers

Challenge pupils to come up with an advantage and a disadvantage for using pyramids of biomass rather than pyramids of numbers. Compare and discuss their ideas.

Misconceptions

Misconception: All pyramids of numbers are pyramid shaped. It is easy for pupils to assume that 'pyramid' diagrams should always be pyramid shapes.

> *Give pupils food chains and ask them to sketch the corresponding 'pyramids' of numbers (they can 'best guess' the appropriate lengths of the bars). Compare and discuss their diagrams. Including examples with trees and parasites will help dispel the misconception that you always have a pyramid shape.*

Misconception: Energy is lost at each trophic level. Very roughly, about ten percent of the energy entering one trophic (feeding) level is passed on to the next. When describing the transfer of energy between trophic levels, many teachers explain that energy is 'lost' to the environment. This implies that the energy has disappeared or been destroyed.

Energy is never 'lost' or destroyed in this sense, but here it may be converted to a less useful form such as heat, which is no longer able to be passed on to the next organism in the chain. Lots of energy is also transferred to the environment from the food chain through excrement and dead bodies. However, this energy is not lost: it can be used by, for example, dung beetles and decomposers such as fungi and bacteria.

Misconception: Plants can be prey. The term prey refers to an **animal** that is eaten by another animal. Plants can therefore not be prey because they are not animals and do not have the ability to move away from danger. Prey often become highly adapted to avoid their potential predators.

> *The snowshoe hare is a prey organism, which has become adapted to detect and escape from danger. Its adaptations include large ears to hear predators coming, eyes on the side of the head for all-round vision and a body structure able to run very fast. It changes the colour of its coat from brown in summer to white in winter, so that it stays camouflaged in its surroundings.*

Misconception: Animals can be prey or predator, but not both. A frog can predate slugs, but also be prey to a snake. Similarly, sparrows may be predators of worms, but prey of a sparrowhawk. Such animals have to display defensive characteristics, so they tend to be less well adapted as predators than top predators (at the end of the food chain) such as lions and eagles.

The use of DDT

DDT (Dichloro-Diphenyl-Trichloroethane) was a commonly used synthetic insecticide. Its use has had both remarkable and devastating effects. Only very small amounts of DDT are needed to kill an insect, but it does not decompose easily and can accumulate to toxic levels in animals and humans.

The accumulation of DDT in birds causes reproductive difficulties. Eggs are produced with thinner shells which break easily and some eggs will not hatch. This caused a dramatic decline in the population of bald eagles in USA in the early 1970s.

year	event
1874	First synthesis.
1939	Insecticidal properties discovered.
WWII	Used successfully to control malaria and lice by killing the mosquito and louse vectors.
1945	Used widely as an agricultural insecticide to increase crop yields.
1948	Paul Hermann Muller was awarded the Nobel Prize in Physiology or Medicine for his discovery that DDT is a very efficient contact poison against several species of arthropod.
1955	World Health Organisation (WHO) programme using DDT to eradicate malaria worldwide. Initially highly successful, eliminating the disease from many countries. Due to the widespread use of DDT in agriculture, many insect populations became resistant.
1962	In 'Silent Spring', Rachel Carson suggested that DDT and other insecticides were a threat to birds and other wildlife. Her book led to a public outcry and contributed to the birth of the environmental movement.
1969	WHO abandoned the programme to eradicate malaria to concentrate on control and treatment of the disease. Spraying programmes were stopped as a result of environmental and safety fears.
1972	Public pressure and a decline in bald eagle populations causes the USA to ban most uses of DDT. Bald eagle populations increased in number soon afterwards.
1984	UK ban on use of DDT.
2004	Agricultural use of DDT banned worldwide under the Stockholm Convention. Limited use today for disease vector control in certain parts of the world remains controversial. In some countries where malaria is a serious health problem, very small quantities of DDT are applied only to the inside walls of houses to kill or repel mosquitoes, so greatly reducing the wider environmental impact.

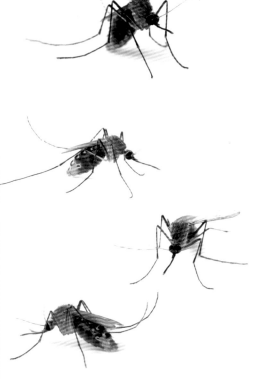

DDT debate

Ask pupils to research and debate the arguments for and against the use of DDT and other insecticides. Are insecticides safe? Are there any situations where the use of DDT is justified?

Reasons why DDT caused devastating environmental problems:

- It is very difficult to break down and persists in an area for many years.
- It is lipid soluble, so is not washed away in the rain but it does dissolve in the body fat of animals, where it becomes concentrated.
- Low levels of DDT in the environment can build up through food chains to lethal concentrations in top predators.
- Predator species are often more badly affected than pest species, so pests can boom when an insecticide is withdrawn, before the controlling predators have had time to recover.

applications and implications

Science at Work

Literacy task

Pupils could be asked to research one species of animal used in biological control. Using their findings, they should produce a fact sheet to explain how the exploitation of this predator-prey relationship brings about control of a pest population without the need for chemicals.

Biological control

Biological control uses natural predators or parasites of pests which reduce crop yields. The technique is most successful when used to control pest populations in closed environments such as greenhouses. Examples include:

- predatory insects such as lacewings will eat many small pests, including spider mites and mealybugs
- parasitoid wasps and flies, such as Braconid wasps used to control greenfly, lay their eggs on or in the body of an insect host which is then eaten by the developing larvae
- moulds such as entomopathogenic fungi commonly used to attack aphids, infect pests with a disease that kills or disables them.

This photograph shows a ladybird eating an aphid (greenfly). Ladybirds are used commercially to control aphid populations when growing tomatoes in greenhouses.

The cane toad – an unwanted guest

The cane toad (*Bufo marinus*) was introduced by the sugar industry into Australia, during the 1930s, to control populations of the French's Cane Beetle and the Greyback Cane Beetle. The larvae of these beetles eat the roots of sugar cane plants, destroying the crop.

Around one hundred toads were originally imported but, within months, the population had exploded to several thousand and continues to spread and grow. The toads:

- are poisonous to humans
- arc poisonous to animals which normally consume frogs or frogs' eggs as part of their natural diet
- compete for food with native fauna
- consume large numbers of honey bees.

Bufo marinus was introduced as a biological control agent. Within five years, an insecticide was developed which was far more effective in controlling beetle populations. Now causing significant damage to the local ecosystem, scientists are looking for ways of controlling this unwanted pest.

> **Controlling the cane toad**
>
> *Ask pupils to research the steps scientists in Australia are taking to control the population of the cane toad Bufo marinus. This includes biological control and gene technology.*

| 14 | organisms and behaviour

the journey so far

During Key Stage 2, pupils should have learnt:
- that some plants lose their leaves in winter
- that some animals hibernate during the winter
- offspring learn behaviour from their parents
- taking drugs can affect a person's behaviour.

the science at key stage 3

Behaviour can be defined as the actions taken by a person, animal or plant in response to internal or external stimuli. A stimulus is any change in the internal or external environment that causes a response. Organisms adopt particular behaviour types because they may increase their chance of survival or their ability to find a mate and reproduce. Some behaviour is innate, others involve learning. Certain chemical substances can cause undesirable changes in behaviour.

Animal responsesn

Learnt responses: All animals have the ability to learn. Learning takes place when behaviour patterns change as the result of experience. Learnt responses tend to be slower, as they are processed by the nervous system. They can be improved by practice. Animals can learn behaviour by observation (for example, a child learns how to talk by copying its parents), trial and error (for example, a cat stung by playing with a bee learns not to play with bees, and possibly any other yellow and black insects) and training (most dogs have 'puppy training classes' to learn to associate basic commands and actions – these are taught by repetition, using a reward such as an edible treat for motivation).

Innate responses: Innate behaviour is automatic and fixed. Newly born animal's responses are for protection or food. To survive, these responses need to take place without learning. For example, newly hatched chicks open their mouths for food from their mother. Reflex actions are also innate responses, for example blinking prevents objects entering the eye. Innate responses are generally very rapid, and occur without conscious thought.

Daily changes

Differences between night and day cause diurnal changes. Most animals sleep during the colder and darker night as it is more difficult to find food or mates. Other species are nocturnal: they sleep during the day and attempt to avoid predators at night. However, nocturnal hunters such as owls and bats have evolved to hunt them. Similarly, twice daily tidal changes affect the behaviour of seashore species such as sea anemones, barnacles and limpets. These feed in water but take action to protect themselves from dessication when exposed to the air. (See *chapter 13: organisms and environment.*)

Seasonal changes

Plant behaviour

Plants also respond to changes in their environment. Deciduous trees, such as the oak or apple, modify their behaviour according to the seasons: spring (new growth is triggered by warmer, lighter days), summer (long warm days allow fruit to develop), autumn (days get colder and shorter, leaves turn brown and fall off), winter (the tree enters a dormant phase).

Animal behaviour

Many animals adapt to seasonal changes. Dogs grow a thicker coat of hair to keep them warm in the winter and shed the extra hair in the spring. Other animals change colour for camouflage. The arctic fox has a red-brown coat during the summer, changing to white during the winter months.

Some animals, such as tortoises, hedgehogs and bears, hibernate during the winter. They retreat into a sheltered place for protection and use the, just enough, food stored in their bodies, to stay alive.

Reacting to the behaviour of others

Courtship behaviour

Animals perform courtship behaviour to attract a partner and produce offspring. This behaviour signals readiness to mate. In some species which only come together to reproduce, courtship behaviour can prevent an aggressive response occurring. At other times an approach may risk injury or even death!

Courtship methods can involve: sound (birds sing to attract mates, crickets 'sing' by rubbing their back legs together and male elks emit a loud 'bugle'); smell (use of chemicals [pheromones] – many female moths and butterflies can attract mates from over six miles away); special characteristics (for example, male deer have large antlers, male peacocks have highly coloured tail feathers and female jumping spiders have ultraviolet reflective body parts, to attract a mate); movement (many animals, such as the male stickleback and the bird of paradise, perform elaborate dances).

Aggressive behaviour

Aggression can occur for a number of reasons – to defend territory, establish dominance within a group or for self defence, for example. Many male animals, such as deer and walruses compete for a harem of females. Animals show aggression in a number of ways. They may produce loud sounds, beat their chest, charge, or ruffle up their feathers to appear larger. Kangaroos 'box' with each other to decide who has the right to mate with a female. Most animals rarely fight their own species as it wastes energy, they risk being killed or injured, and time is wasted which could be used for finding food.

Human behaviour can be affected by drugs

A drug is a chemical substance which can alter body functions. Some affect behaviour by altering the brain's responses to stimuli. Such drugs can relax the body or remove pain and also make people more energetic. Stimulants, such as cocaine and caffeine, speed up the nervous system and increase brain activity. Depressants (sedatives), such as tranquillisers and alcohol, slow down the nervous system and decrease brain activity.

In addiction, the body adjusts to drug use and becomes dependent on it for normal functioning. Nicotine in cigarettes causes smoking addiction. A person addicted to a substance will suffer unpleasant withdrawal symptoms when they try to give it up. (See *chapter 10: staying healthy*.)

the journey ahead

During Key Stage 4, pupils will learn about behaviour in greater detail. They will study:

- how drugs can cause both beneficial and damaging effects on the body
- how reflex reactions differ from controlled reactions
- how nerve impulses are transmitted along nerves and across synapses.

This topic is studied in much greater detail in courses with psychology components.

teaching issues

When to teach this topic

This material can be taught as a discrete topic or split up, to be taught within other topics. For example, courtship can form part of the reproduction topic and seasonal changes could be taught as part of adaptations.

Misconceptions

Misconception: Only animal behaviour is affected by daily changes. Many plant species react to diurnal changes. Daisies close their petals at night. This is thought to conserve the attractant chemicals of the flower when there are no pollinators around. Some species also close up their leaves at night time, possibly to conserve water.

The daisy's name originates from the phrase 'days eye', which refers to the fact that daisies open during the day and close at night.

Misconception: Hibernation is to escape the cold. Most animals do hibernate (enter a deep state of sleep) to escape the cold, and this is true of warm blooded hibernators, with the one exception of the Malagasy fat-tailed dwarf lemur! This, and certain cold blooded hibernators, do so to escape the heat. The scientific term for this behaviour is aestivation. Cold blooded animals, such as reptiles like crocodiles, have a body temperature the same as their environment. In hot conditions a reptile's body temperature may rise up to 43 degrees Celsius. In order to survive the hot dry conditions and lack of water, some reptiles, amphibians, insects and snails aestivate underground.

Misconception: Caffeine and alcohol are not drugs. Many pupils think of drugs as medicines or illegal substances. Many pupils are unaware that coffee, tea and cola contain caffeine, and that caffeine alters the function of the mind and body and so is a drug. Although the mind-altering properties of alcohol will be known, many will not consider it to be a drug.

Closing flowers

Set pupils homework to discover which plants close their flowers or leaves at night, by looking in gardens at dusk. Organise them in teams and see who found the most examples.

Literacy task

Ask pupils to carry out some research into how a particular species hibernates. Do they need to collect a store of food? Do they have to store additional fat in the body? What happens to their body's metabolic processes whilst they are asleep? Pupils could share their findings with the class with short presentations or posters.

Caffeine investigations

Challenge pupils to design investigations into the effects of caffeine as a stimulant. They might look at the effect on reaction times after drinking a cup of cola or Red Bull. Plans should be vetted and risk assessments made before investigations are tried out. This can lead to discussions of: the nature of drugs and their actions, including side effects and addiction, how to choose sample sizes, and the problems of drug trials, including placebo effects and double blind trials.

Note: check for caffeine-sensitive pupils – they can act as 'referees' to check designs.

Misconception: Legal drugs are harmless. Many pupils believe that:

- recreational drugs such as alcohol are harmless because they are freely available to adults
- over the counter drugs such as pain killers are harmless because you can buy them in shops
- prescription drugs such as sleeping tablets are harmless because they are prescribed by a doctor.

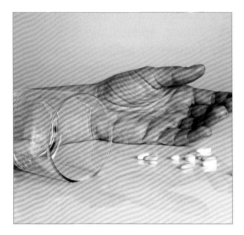

Often, drug takers find they have to increase their dose for a drug to continue to have the same effect. This is because their body has developed a tolerance to the drug. This can result in taking a larger dose than their body can cope with – an overdose, which can be fatal.

Misconception: You can't teach an old dog new tricks. The phrase 'you can't teach an old dog new tricks' suggests that learning stops after a certain age. Learning, including in dogs, occurs throughout life. Any pet can be trained at any age and very old people are able to learn new skills and pass exams. However, both humans and dogs are easier to train when younger because they do not have to unlearn so many previously learnt bad habits.

OTC medicines

Pupils can be provided with information leaflets found in over the counter medicines such as pain killers, cold and cough remedies and antihistamines, to discuss the significance of the information provided. They could work in small groups, with each group preparing a short presentation for one example.

Adult learners

Conduct a quick survey to find out if any pupils have older relatives or family friends who are taking courses or learning new skills. Examples could be a foreign language, new skills for their job or skills for a retirement hobby.

---

applications and implications

Science at Work

Studying the brain

To understand the brain's structure and function, scientists in the past mapped the brain using evidence from stroke victims. In a stroke, blood vessels in a localised region of the brain become blocked or leak causing damage of varying severity. Matching the damaged region to the effects, such as loss of movement of a limb, has enabled scientists to work out the functions of different regions of the brain.

Further evidence has come from using electrical impulses from electrodes placed in specific parts of animal brains to stimulate observable responses, such as movement. Research has also taken place during human brain surgery. As the brain has no pain receptors, surgeons have been able to obtain feedback from conscious patients on the sensations that they are experiencing.

More intricate details of the brain are being gained using neuro-imaging techniques such as functional magnetic resonance imaging (fMRI) and electroencephalography (EEG).

EEG has been used to study changes in electrical activity of the brain, for example during sleep. However, more recently, really exciting advances have been made using neuro-imaging techniques, such as fMRI. This is now the method of choice for learning how a normal, injured or diseased brain is working. It is possible to map brain activity in detail and determine precisely which part of the brain is handling functions such as thinking, speech, movement and vision. Brain damage caused by a stroke or a disease and the related changes in brain function can be very accurately assessed.

The main parts of the brain and their functions

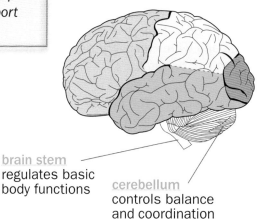

frontal lobe: personality; emotions; motor skills; problem solving; reasoning

parietal lobe: sensory

temporal lobe: language; hearing; speech

occipital lobe: vision

brain stem
regulates basic body functions

cerebellum
controls balance and coordination

history and culture

Early studies of the brain

On September 13 1848, aged 25, American Phineas Gage blasted an iron rod through his skull and brain ... and survived!

Gage was using explosive charges to remove rock for the construction of a railway. Long, narrow holes were drilled into the rock and filled with gunpowder. On this occasion Gage forgot to add a protective barrier of sand. When packing down the gunpowder with a metre long, thirty millimetre diameter iron tamping rod, he created a spark. The subsequent explosion propelled the rod through the bottom of his left cheekbone and out through the top of his head, landing almost thirty metres behind him.

Workmates found Gage slumped on the ground with a hole through his skull, but he was still alive and breathing. Within moments he opened his eyes and began speaking. His colleagues loaded him into a cart, and took him to his house forty five minutes away.

When Doctor John Harlow arrived, Gage was still conscious, had a regular heartbeat, and both of his pupils reacted to light normally. He was reported to be 'in full possession of his reason, and free from pain'. A few days later, Gage's exposed brain became infected and Harlow had to drain around 250 cm³ of pus from an abscess under his skull. Amazingly, after ten weeks, Gage recovered enough to be sent home.

During his recovery, Harlow noted some changes in his personality. Several months later Gage was fit enough to work, but due to his personality changes, his previous employers would not employ him in the same position. This resulted in Gage taking various jobs caring for horses, driving stagecoaches, and doing some farm work. Eleven years after the accident, Gage began to experience epileptic seizures. He died several months later, on 21 May 1860 aged 37.

In 1868, Dr. Harlow documented the "mental manifestations" of Gage's brain injuries in a report published in the Bulletin of the Massachusetts Medical Society. Harlow wrote that "*Gage was fitful, irreverent, indulging at times in the grossest profanity (which was not previously his custom), manifesting but little deference for his fellows, impatient of restraint or advice when it conflicts with his desires, at times pertinaciously obstinate, yet capricious and vacillating, devising many plans of future operations, which are no sooner arranged than they are abandoned in turn for others appearing more feasible. A child in his intellectual capacity and manifestations, he has the animal passions of a strong man. Previous to his injury, although untrained in the schools, he possessed a well-balanced mind, and was looked upon by those who knew him as a shrewd, smart businessman, very energetic and persistent in executing all his plans of operation. In this regard his mind was radically changed, so decidedly that his friends and acquaintances said he was 'no longer Gage'.*"

The case of Gage had considerable influence on nineteenth century understanding of the brain. It provided evidence of localisation of functions, and showed that damage to specific regions such as the frontal lobes could alter aspects of personality and affect social skills.

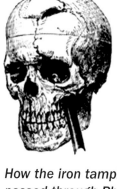

How the iron tamping rod passed through Phineas Gage's skull

Pavlov's dogs

Dogs naturally produce saliva as a response to the sight and smell of food. This is a completely automatic reflex action. The food is an unconditioned stimulus, and the act of salivation is an unconditioned response.

During the 1890s, Russian scientist Ivan Pavlov – while carrying out research into the physiology of digestion in dogs – noticed that dogs would salivate even when they couldn't see or smell food. Rather, they began to salivate when they saw the lab technician who normally fed them. The dogs did not want to eat this person! Instead, they now unconciously *associated* the lab technician with the presence of food, automatically causing them to salivate.

Ivan Pavlov

Cartoon conditioning

Ask pupils to produce a cartoon to illustrate Pavlov's famous conditioning experiment, showing the original unconditioned response, the training and the new conditioned response. Alternatively, you could ask them to research J B Watson's famous experiment with 'Little Albert' and illustrate it in the same way.

Pavlov tested this theory with his most famous experiment. He rang a bell every time the dogs were fed. Eventually, the dogs associated the sound of the bell with food. Sure enough, the dogs would now salivate at the sound of the bell, even when they could neither see nor smell food.

The bell was a conditioned stimulus, the salivation to the sound of the bell was a conditioned response.

Forming connections in this way is called conditioning.

Instinctive responses

The term 'Pavlov's dog' is used to refer to someone who responds predictably on instinct or through a conditioned response, rather than someone who has a reasoned response to a situation.

Ask pupils to come up with situations which could illustrate this.

For example, the smell of an anti-bacterial product might make a person feel sick if it was used in their childhood to clean up after an episode of vomiting.

Many phobias are thought to be conditioned responses, where a harmless stimulus has been associated with a frightening event.

On a lighter note, if your school uses bells to signal the end of lessons, it is likely that everyone will salivate to the lunchtime bell!

hot topics

Cannibalism and intensively farmed hens

Cannibalistic behaviour occurs sporadically throughout the animal kingdom, in both the wild and captivity. In the wild, it can be viewed as a form of adaptation – it removes weaker organisms reducing competition, as well as providing nutrients. In captivity, however, it is perceived as abnormal, and is a sign that an animal is in distress.

Cannibalism in intensively farmed hens creates economic and welfare issues for poultry farmers. The reasons why it occurs are not fully understood, but factors which increase the amount of cannibalism include:

- a high density of birds, within a confined area
- an inability to forage
- the presence of small or weak chicks
- restriction of food or water intake
- a diet lacking in protein
- exposing birds to light that is too intense.

Battery hens

Ask pupils to carry out research into the farming techniques used for intensively and organically-reared, egg-laying chickens. From their research, pupils should write a well-reasoned essay on which type of farming they support. The essay should include both animal welfare and economic information.

Note: battery cages are due to be banned in the EU from 2012 and replaced by enriched cages.

Previously caged birds, which are farmed in a free-range environment, do not tend to display cannibalistic tendencies. The solution used in intensive poultry farms is to de-beak birds when they are a few days old.

Attention Deficit Hyperactivity Disorder (ADHD)

Children with ADHD have difficulty functioning in the home, at school, and with their peers. Three of the most common behaviours exhibited are:

1. Impulsiveness – acting quickly without thinking first.
2. Hyperactivity – struggling to sit still; may involve walking, running or climbing around a room when others are seated, and talking when others are talking.
3. Inattention – regularly daydreaming, and being easily sidetracked from a task.

For decades, ADHD has been treated with medication. The drugs used depend on the child and their age, but all fall into the category of stimulants. A common drug used with school age children is Ritalin. Recently there has been a move to try and treat ADHD sufferers with behaviour management techniques. In many cases a combination of both treatments is most successful.

ADHD fact sheet

Ask pupils to produce a fact sheet about the advantages and disadvantages of treating children with ADHD with drugs such as Ritalin. The fact sheet should be aimed at parents and teenage children who wish to play an active role in deciding on the best course of treatment for their child or themselves.

---

useful data

The unit system used here is the International System of Units (SI Units). This is the modern version of the metric system. Although SI is the most commonly used unit system, other unit systems are also used, for example Imperial (units include pints, inches and pounds). Units named after people start with a lower case letter when written out in full, but a capital when abbreviated.

SI Base units

quantity	SI unit	symbol
amount of substance	mole	mol
electric current	ampere	A
length	metre	m
luminous intensity	candela	cd
mass	kilogram	kg
temperature	kelvin	K
time	second	s

plane angle	radian	rad
solid angle	steradian	sr

Some derived and other units

quantity	base SI units	derived unit	symbol
acceleration	$m\ s^{-2}$		
area	m^2		
volume	m^3		
concentration	$mol\ m^{-3}$		
	$mol\ dm^{-3}$		
density	$kg\ m^{-3}$		
electrical potential difference	$kg\ m^2\ A^{-1}\ s^{-3}$	volt	V
electrical resistance	$kg\ m^2\ A^{-2}\ s^{-3}$	ohm	Ω
energy	$kg\ m^2\ s^{-2}$	joule	J
force	$kg\ m\ s^{-2}$	newton	N
power	$kg\ m^2\ s^{-3}$	watt	W
pressure	$kg\ m^{-1}\ s^{-2}$	pascal	Pa
		millimetres of mercury	mm Hg
speed	$m\ s^{-1}$		
acceleration	$m\ s^{-2}$		
momentum	$kg\ m\ s^{-1}$		
frequency	s^{-1}	hertz	Hz
radioactivity	s^{-1}	becquerel	Bq
temperature	K	degrees Celsius	^0C
magnetic field strength	$A\ m^{-1}$		

Some common conversions between units

metric		imperial	imperial		metric
1 centimetre	10 mm	0.3937 inch	1 inch		2.54 cm
1 metre	1000 mm	1.0936 yards	1 yard	3 feet	0.9144 m
1 kilometre	1000 m	0.6214 miles	1 mile	1760 yards	1.6093 km
			1 nautical mile	2025.4 yards	1.852 km
1 light year	9.4605×10^{12} km	5.8785×10^{12} miles			
1 m^2	10 000 cm^2	1.1960 square yards	1 yd^2	9 square feet	0.8361 m^2
1 hectare	1 ha / 10 000 m^2	2.4710 acres	1 acre	4840 yd^2	4046.9 m^2
1 square km	1 km^2 / 100 ha				
1 cubic cm	1 cm^3	0.0610 cubic inch	1 in^3		16.3870 cm^3
1 cubic dm	1 dm^3 / 1000 cm^3				
1 litre	1 dm^3	1.7598 pint	1 pint	20 fluid ounces	0.5683 dm^3
1 cubic metre	1 m^3 / 1000 dm^3	1.3080 cubic yards			
			1 gallon	8 pints	4.5461 dm^3
			1 gallon	1.2010 US gallons	
1 kilogram	1000 g	2.2046 pound	1 lb	16 ounces	0.4536 kg
			1 stone	14 lb	6.3504 kg
1 tonne	1 t / 1000 kg	0.9842 ton (long UK)	1 ton	20 cwt	1.0160 t
1 kg m^{-3}	0.001 g cm^{-3}				
1 km/h	0.2778 m s^{-1}	0.6214 miles per hour	1 mph	0.8690 knots	1.6093 km/hour
1 m s^{-1}	3.6 km/hour				
1 Pa	1 N m^{-2} 1 kg m^{-1} s^{-2} 0.0075 mmHg ($\cong$ mtorr) 0.0100 millibar (mbar)	0.0001 pound force per square inch (psi)	1 psi		6.8948 kPa

SI prefixes

10^{18}		exa	E	10^{-1}	0.1	deci	d
10^{15}		peta	P	10^{-2}	0.01	centi	c
10^{12}		tera	T	10^{-3}	0.001	milli	m
10^{9}	1 000 000 000	giga	G	10^{-6}	0.000 001	micro	μ
10^{6}	1 000 000	mega	M	10^{-9}	0.000 000 001	nano	n
10^{3}	1000	kilo	K	10^{-12}		pico	p
10^{2}	100	hecto	H	10^{-15}		femto	f
10		deca	da	10^{-18}		atto	a

typical lengths

name	symbol	length / m	
terametre	Tm	10^{12}	bigger than the diameter of the solar system, less than the distance to the closest star
gigametre	Gm	10^{9}	the Sun is 1.5 Gm across
megametre	Mm	10^{6}	diameter of the Earth – 12.8 Mm
kilometre	km	10^{3}	Angel Falls, Venezuela – 980 metres
hectometre	hm	10^{2}	length of football pitch
decametre	dm	10	orca (or killer whale)
metre	m	1	royal python snake
centimetre	cm	10^{-2}	width of a fingernail
millimetre	mm	10^{-3}	mite
micrometre	μm	10^{-6}	bacterium
nanometre	nm	10^{-9}	buckyball (buckminsterfullerene) – approximately 1 nm
picometre	pm	10^{-12}	atom diameters range from 30–600 pm

typical temperatures

	approximate value / °C
Large Hadron Collider	-271
embryo storage	-196
South Pole average	-48
whole blood storage	<6
bovine semen storage	17
hypothermia	<35
human body (oral)	37
fluorescent light	70
medical autoclave	>121
Bunsen burner flame	1300
surface of the Sun	5800
lightning	30 000

typical masses

	approximate value / kg
electron	9×10^{-31}
hydrogen atom	1.7×10^{-27}
small virus	10^{-17}
E. coli bacterium	6.7×10^{-15}
grain of sand	10^{-7}
mouse	3.5×10^{-2}
1 dm^3 water	1
average adult human	70
male African elephant	7×10^3
blue whale	10^5
giant sequoia tree	6×10^6
the Moon	7×10^{22}
the Earth	6×10^{24}
the Sun	2×10^{30}
milky way galaxy	2×10^{42}

renewable and non-renewable resources

renewable resources		non-renewable resources	
· everlasting supply of energy		· once used they cannot be replaced	
· will not run out		· they will eventually run out	
biofuels	**the Sun**	**fossil fuels**	**nuclear fuels**
· wood	· solar energy	· coal	
· straw	**water**	· oil	
· oil from plants	· hydroelectric power	· natural gas	
· sugar and starch	· waves		
· biogas	· tides		
	wind		

human classification

Kingdom	Animalia
Phylum	Chordata
Class	Mammalia
Order	Primates
Infraorder	Catarrhini
Superfamily	Hominoidea
Family	Hominidae
Genus	Homo
Species	*Homo sapiens*
Sub-species	*Homo sapiens sapiens*

charges on biologically-important common ions

charge	positive ions	
1+	copper(I)	Cu^+
	hydrogen	H^+
	potassium	K^+
	silver	Ag^+
	sodium	Na^+
2+	calcium	Ca^{2+}
	copper(II)	Cu^{2+}
	iron(II)	Fe^{2+}
	lead(II)	Pb^{2+}
	magnesium	Mg^{2+}
	zinc	Zn^{2+}
3+	aluminium	Al^{3+}
	iron (III)	Fe^{3+}

charge	positive ions	
1–	chloride	Cl^-
	hydrogen carbonate	HCO_3^-
	hydroxide	OH^-
	iodide	I^-
	nitrate	NO^-
	nitrite	NO^-
2–	carbonate	CO_3^{2-}
	oxide	O^{2-}
	sulfate	SO_4^{2-}
	sulfite	SO_3^{2-}
3–	phosphate	PO_4^{2-}

typical forces

	newtons
electron - proton force in hydrogen atom	10^{-8}
weight of 2p piece	0.07
weight of a blackbird	1.1
one kilogram	9.81
average weight of newborn baby	34.5
human biting force	200 – 1200
weight of average adult	700
karate chop	1000

density of common materials

	kg m^{-3}		kg m^{-3}
air*	1.29	milk (15 °C)	1040
ash	705	nitrogen*	1.25
apple	640	oak	760
barley	640	oats (rolled)	300
beans (cocoa)	590	oxygen*	1.43
beeswax	960	pine	500
bone	1910	potatoes	770
butter	870	salt (table)	1200
carbon dioxide*	1.98	sand	1601
clay	2160	snow (compacted)	480
coconut oil	0.93	soil	1200-2000
coffee (fresh beans)	560	sugar solution	68
cork	240	sugar (granulated)	850
ebony	1190	sunflower oil (20 °C)	920
flour (wheat)	590	teak	657
hydrogen*	0.09	water (pure)	1000
ice	920	water (sea – 25 °C)	1020
ivory	1870	water vapour*	0.80
lard	948	wheat grain	800
leather	961	wool	1300
maize	760	* all at 0 °C and 1 atm pressure	
methane*	0.72		

index

other books in this series

chemical and material behaviour

contents

energy, electricity and forces

contents

the environment, earth and universe

contents

interpreting how science works

contents

Also available from 4science